RACIST INCIDENTS AND BULLYING IN SCHOOLS

How to prevent them and how to respond when they happen

RACIST INCIDENTS AND BULLYING IN SCHOOLS

How to prevent them and how to respond when they happen

Principles, guidance and good practice

Robin Richardson and Berenice Miles

Trentham Books

Stoke on Trent, UK and Sterling, USA

Trentham Books Limited

Westview House 22883 Quicksilver Drive
734 London Road Sterling
Oakhill VA 20166-2012
Stoke on Trent USA
Staffordshire
England ST4 5NP

First published 2008

British Library Cataloguing-in-Publication Data
A catalogue record for this book is available from the British Library

ISBN: 978 1 85856 428 9

Designed and typeset by Trentham Print Design Ltd, Chester and printed in Great Britain by Page Bros (Norwich) Ltd.

CONTENTS

INTRODUCTORY

1

Unkind names at school
An episode and issues arising

'Anybody who was ever called unkind names at school,' said an editorial comment in *The Daily Telegraph* on Saturday 8 April 2006, 'must be gasping with astonishment this weekend.'

Having caught its readers' attention, the editorial explained it was referring to the news in the previous day's paper (Britten, 2006) that the Crown Prosecution Service (CPS) had 'thought fit to bring criminal charges against a 10-year-old who is said to have called an 11-year-old schoolmate a 'Paki' and 'Bin Laden' in the playground.' The paper quoted with warm approval the district court judge who was hearing the case at Salford Youth Court in Greater Manchester:

> 'I was repeatedly called fat at school,' said the judge. 'Does this amount to a criminal offence? ... Nobody is more against racist abuse than me, but these are boys in a playground, this is nonsense... There must be other ways of dealing with this apart from criminal prosecution. In the old days, the headmaster would have got them both and given them a good clouting.' The judge had other home truths to tell, which ought to give the Greater Manchester Police and the CPS pause for thought. 'This is how stupid the whole system is getting,' he said. 'There are major crimes out there and the police don't bother to prosecute. If you get your car stolen, it doesn't matter, but you get two kids falling out ... this is nonsense.'

'Two kids falling out ... this is nonsense'. This was the recurring refrain in most other papers commenting on the same story. There had been a playground tiff, scrap, jibe, argument, taunt, minor disagreement, quarrel or squabble – all these terms were used – involving two individuals. It had not been serious, merely the typical behaviour of young children. 'Up on a charge of being a typical child,' said a headline in the *Sunday Times* (9 April). 'It happens all the time', declared editorial comment in the *Daily Mail* (8 April). It continued:

> Schoolchildren squabble. There may be tears. They call each other utterly un-acceptable names. Their teacher calls them over and tells them not to be so offen-sive and learn to respect each other. So children learn to become responsible adults. Not this time. Now a playground quarrel engages the full majesty of the law, with a police investigation, a file prepared for the Crown Prosecution Service, an appearance in court ...

The district judge, commented the *Mail*, was 'splendid'. Spokespersons for the NUT and the NASUWT, however, robustly denounced him. This brought upon them personal and sexist abuse from the conservative press. In the *Sunday Telegraph* (9 April), A.N.Wilson claimed the case was about a 10-year-old boy 'calling another little boy rude names'; and that 'it can't be long before the hags and thought-police of the teachers' unions try to outlaw the use of nicknames altogether'. (The 'nicknames' in the present case, it was reported in some papers, included not only Paki and Bin Laden but also Nigger, as in 'He is on the run, pull the trigger and shoot the nigger, five, four, three, two, one'.) An article in the *Mail* (Slack and Narain, 2006) quoted an anonymous former colleague of the general secretary of the NASUWT to the effect that 'she can be too blinkered and inflexible. I'm not sure she knows when to settle and that gets people's backs up. I think she's difficult to get on with.' Editorial comment in the *Mail* on the same day referred to her 'politically correct world of inverted values'. 'If this kind of sanctimonious silliness exists at the top of the teachers' unions', wondered Minette Marrin in the *Sunday Times*, 'what hope is there for education in this country?' The entire episode, she said, had 'a faint whiff of the Soviet show trials or the Salem witch-hunts about it, a kind of public hysteria. Whom the gods wish to destroy, they first make mad.'

Similarly trenchant criticisms of the unions came from the British National Party (BNP), which contrasted the judge's 'common sense statements' with 'the real bully boys and girls, the hate-filled Marxists of the National Union of Teachers'. Simon Heffer in the *Telegraph*, under the heading 'Racists: we've got to catch them young', asserted that the statements by the unions reflected 'their crazed desire to stalinise our children rather than educate them' and commended 'the abundant common sense' of the judge in saying that 'what the boy required, at most, was a clip round the ear'. He concluded with pon-derous sarcasm:

> Since neither the CPS nor the police have anything better to do, perhaps I could suggest an extension of this policy, starting with abandoning the minimum age of

criminality. It is obvious that all primary schools and, indeed, nurseries should be regularly inspected for signs of racist tots, with exemplary prosecutions where necessary. And don't forget maternity wards – you can't catch them too young, and heaven knows what harm is being done to our nation by bigoted babies.

Sarcasm and denial along these lines were also expressed on the websites of the *Mail* and *Telegraph* in summer 2008 when a book on racism amongst young children was published (Lane, 2008) and on the website of the *Guardian* when the book's authors defended it (Ouseley and Lane, 2008).

In relation to the Salford case in 2006, the BNP blamed 'self-loathing white advocates of multiculturalism' and Carole Malone in the *Sunday Mirror* (9 April), under the headline 'Shame on the playtime police', blamed 'lentil-eating liberals who ... refuse to believe anyone is intrinsically evil'. Ann Widdecombe, under the heading 'Don't take playground tiffs into the courtroom' (*Daily Express*, 12 April), reflected that 'the country is well nigh paralysed by political correctness, fear of giving offence and the compensation culture'. She added: 'It is a pity the head could not apply the slipper, as the judge acknowledged.' Her conclusion was to do with malaise in the state of Britain as a whole, not just about '10-year-olds being rude in the playground', and was a scattergun attack on a wide range of targets:

> Truly the lunatics have taken over the asylum. Truly I understand why people emigrate. My only surprise is that there is anybody left here at all. The NHS is in a state of near collapse, education has become a joke, the law-abiding live behind bars as they fortify their houses, pension schemes have been robbed by the most irresponsible Chancellor I can remember, the countryside is full of useless devices which wave their arms around and produce scarcely enough energy to propel a toy train and 10-year-olds are prosecuted for being rude in the playground.

A Muslim dimension of the affair was indicated by the terms Bin Laden and Paki in the insults that were alleged to have been used, and in the *Daily Mail* (8 April 2006) by the inclusion of a quotation from the chair of the Muslim Council of Britain's education committee, who had said: 'We need to be sensible in relation to 10-year-old children. The issue of racism is, of course, very serious but we should educate them, not take them to court.' The *Mail* commented that 'to its credit, the Muslim Council of Britain sees this affair for what it is and says the case should never have come to court'. It contrasted this with 'the bovine, brainwashed, politically-correct mindset of the liberal establishment'. 'The only good news in this sorry story', it was said in the *Sunday Times*, 'is that the Muslim Council of Britain has taken a wise and adult line, sensitive though Muslims are to racism. It has supported the judge in his comments.'

It is sobering to compare the news coverage outlined above with an account of what actually happened. It was the *Mail on Sunday* that took the trouble to find out and to publish the facts. An article by Andrew Chapman and Louisa Pritchard (9 April) explained the background. In a nutshell, the episode under consideration had not been a playground spat, tiff or squabble, but had involved persistent bullying and physical attacks over several months. It had not been a single child doing the bullying, but three. The police and the CPS had *not* taken the case to court on a whim, but had used restorative justice approaches to try to persuade the three alleged offenders to accept reprimands or warnings; they had been successful with two of them but not with the third, which was why the third had had to come to court.

The article was based on an interview with the mother of the boy who had been at the receiving end of the bullying. 'I was disgusted,' she said, 'by the judge's remarks, that seemed to belittle my son's ordeal even further'. She continued:

> The judge is wrong. He may have been fat at school and he may have been called names. But my son can never change the colour of his skin and that's the difference here. I just wish the judge had seen the tears streaming down my son's face when he finally broke down and told me all about what had happened to him. How dare the judge match being called fat in the same vein as the racist abuse my son has had to suffer? I was angered by his comments. This has not just been a one-off name-calling session, this has amounted to several months of systematic taunting and bullying which has left my child withdrawn and miserable. Some of the names he has been called would make your hair curl.

Her son, she continued, 'was in a terrible state – withdrawn, sulky and upset. It was very cruel and humiliating. He'd never encountered anything like this before. The school was magnificent throughout and tried to deal with what was happening through normal disciplinary channels.'

The *Mail on Sunday* article also quoted from a statement by the CPS:

> We originally decided the case did not need to be brought before the courts, and an official reprimand by the police was offered to the three boys. In one case a reprimand was accepted and given, in another a final warning was given because he had already had a reprimand for another matter but the third boy, although he admitted some of the offence, would not accept the reprimand after his parents took legal advice.

In due course, before the case came back to court, the third accused did accept a warning and the case was dropped. The Chief Crown Prosecutor for Greater Manchester issued a statement that politely but assertively challenged the judge and indicated the latter accepted he had been mistaken:

[The judge] made remarks about the decision to prosecute which were highly critical of the CPS. He was not aware of the full history of the matter, in particular the prior disposal of the allegations against the other two boys. He has accepted that he may well have been less forthright in his comments if he had been aware.

The judge also apologised in writing to the chief constable of Greater Manchester Police, Michael Todd, for the criticisms of the police he had made in court (BBC News, 26 April 2006). These admissions by the judge of ignorance and hasty judgement on his own part received no mention in the conservative press. On the contrary, the withdrawal of the charges was reported as 'a victory for common sense' (Narain, 2006, see also Bunyan, 2006), implying it was the common sense of the CPS that had prevailed rather than, as had in fact been the case, the common sense of the alleged culprit's parents, and whoever was advising them. The story was kept in cuttings files in its incomplete and uncorrected form, however, and surfaced again in summer 2008, with the additional false embellishment that the case had been dropped as a result of a direct order by the judge (Doughty, 2008). In years to come it may acquire additional embellishments whenever it is trotted out in the media to illustrate concerns about so-called political correctness and the state of British society. It already has the features of an urban legend, one that will run and run.

For the conservative media, the episode was not *just* an episode. It was also, to use a metaphor developed by theorists specialising in conflict resolution and transformation (Lederach, 2003), an epicentre – it drew attention, in their view, to seismic tensions, shifts and crises beneath the surface of society. These were summarised as being to do with political correctness, but the real anxieties arguably went rather deeper, and were to do with irrevocable social, economic and political changes amounting to 'the unsettling of Britain' (Commission on the Future of Multi-Ethnic Britain, 2000:23) such as globalisation, loss of Empire, devolution of decision-making power, moral and social pluralism, decline of national influence, post-war migration and closeness to the rest of Europe. Be that as it may, this book on dealing with racist bullying and incidents in schools touches frequently on the wider social context within which schools operate.

The book honours the school in Greater Manchester that was 'magnificent throughout' and, more generally, the leaders of the teaching unions who risked the wrath of the conservative press by speaking out for their members against the judge in the case described. Amongst other things, the book's purpose is to embolden teachers to withstand the cruel simplicities, slurs and slogans of the conservative press, and to educate their pupils accordingly.

The pattern of the book is as follows. First (chapter 2), there is an account of racist bullying and incidents in schools as seen by those at the receiving end. The mother quoted above described how racist behaviour by other children had caused her son to be 'in a terrible state – withdrawn, sulky and upset'. It is essential that action and policies against racism in schools should be informed and inspired by the experiences, stories and perceptions of those who suffer most. It is relevant to note that, with the single exception in *The Mail on Sunday*, no newspapers tried to report the case from the point of view of the boy who had been targeted, hurt and harmed.

Chapter 3 deals with basic concepts. The judge in the Salford case, as also the journalists who supported him, showed substantial ignorance and insensitivity. Such ignorance is rare amongst members of the teaching profession. Teachers do, however, need to be able to respond robustly and confidently to the kinds of attitude and ignorance displayed by the judge and the right-wing commentators. In particular the chapter is concerned with clarifying definitions and vocabulary.

The next two chapters are to do with dealing with incidents that occur. Chapter 4 discusses four broad approaches and characterises these as dismissive, punitive, corrective and transformative. The dismissive approach is the one adopted by the judge in the Salford case – 'two kids falling out', with the implication that there was nothing much to worry about. The punitive approach was also advocated by the judge: 'In the old days, the headmaster would have got them both and given them a good clouting'. The corrective approach involves teaching facts and intellectual arguments. Punitive and corrective approaches have their uses, but what essentially is required, chapter 4 argues, is an approach that can appropriately be described as restorative or transformative.

Chapter 5 discusses practical and theoretical issues around the recording and reporting of incidents.

The rest of the book is about prevention. There are discussions of key ideas across the curriculum (chapter 6); teaching about emotive and controversial histories, for example around the transatlantic slave trade (chapter 7); classroom activities about antiracism in popular culture, particularly football (chapter 8); the uses of drama and theatre in empowering children and young people to be active citizens in opposing racism, and not mere bystanders (chapter 9); teaching about distortions and simplifications in the media of the kind that have been highlighted in this introductory overview of the book's content and concerns (chapter 10); and the continuing professional development of staff (chapter 11). The chapter on professional development, it is relevant to note here as a kind of foretaste, is about hearts as well as minds and about, in the words of a speaker at one of the national conferences that led indirectly to this book, 'love and care and concern and kindness'.

Concluding note

The composer Nitin Sawhney enjoyed his schooldays by and large, and had the good fortune to meet some inspirational teachers. 'But I went through school,' he writes, 'with an uneasy suspicion that I was inferior'. He wondered why:

> It may have been a product of the notion that the history of the non-white population of this world is embedded in slavery and colonisation, or perhaps the echoing resonance of the word Paki as it accompanied me through the hostile corridors of the science block. (Sawhney, 2004:34)

Sawhney beautifully crystallises in this sentence the twin concerns of this book. On the one hand, it is concerned with challenging and seeking to demolish the hostile corridors of the science block, and all such places where young people interact outside the supervision of adults and where a traumatic experience may be the echoing resonance of the word Paki, and similar abusive, excluding, devastating words and actions. The book is also about school classrooms, and what is taught and learnt there about history and humanity, and about so-called race. Corridors and classrooms can reinforce each other, as did those which Sawhney encountered, to give out the message that certain human beings are inferior. Alternatively, corridors and classrooms can reinforce each other with the opposite message: all are equal and all belong, though all are different. All have key roles not only in demolishing hostile corridors and curricula but also in replacing them with alternatives, and keeping the alternatives in good repair, day by day.

The book is about much more, that is to say, than 'unkind names at school'. Its first main chapter after this introduction, as mentioned above, involves listening at length to the voices and views of children and young people. Listen to us, they say: we are the experts, we have a right to be listened to.

UNDERSTANDING

2

Right to be listened to
Voices, views and stories from young people

'I don't know a single black person who hasn't been attacked at least verbally, and most physically' ... 'The teachers are mostly white. You can't look at a white person and tell if they are a racist, so if they haven't told you their views you can't go to a white person and complain about white racism' ... ... 'We would like teachers to know that racism does happen and that teachers should confront bullies about the matter' ... 'Teachers need to be aware that there's problems after school and at lunchtime' ... 'Teachers need to know how it feels to be told a racist comment and how we feel about bullying' ... 'I have the right for no-one to be unkind to me because of my colour or religion' ... 'I have the right to be listened to'.

Except for a few attributed quotes, the views and voices quoted here were collected between 2002 and 2007 in focus group meetings, individual meetings, two conferences and a series of workshops with young people aged from 5 to 18. No questionnaires were used, and there was no adult direction which might have mediated a particular type of response. Raw hurt and pain come through the quotations, as do wisdom, compassion, humanity and a passion for justice. The chapter affirms the generous nature and good sense of children and young people, exposes their experience and pain and casts light on the reasons why, in general, white adults in schools are not aware of what is happening. The chapter is for those who are willing to listen and learn and accept. It is written in the belief that children's voices are powerful, perceptive and passionate. They must not be ignored.

Statements and charters of rights

Children and young people want to learn in cohesive school communities, free from racism and bullying. In a series of workshops pupils aged 5-18 from multiethnic inner-city schools arrived at the statement below:

> We want a school where *all* pupils look out for each other.
>
> We all have the right to learn in a safe, peaceful environment free from victimisation and fear. We will not tolerate any form of racist bullying, whether it is by calling people names, threatening them or hurting them in any way. We know our rights and responsibilities and we will work together to protect them for ourselves and others.
>
> We want a school where all pupils can be proud of themselves and their cultures, and of each other.

In the workshops, pupils in key stage 1 prepared a charter of rights for key stage 1 and nurseries:

- I have the right to be treated the same as everyone else: nicely, kindly, fairly.
- I have the right for no-one to be unkind to me because of my colour or religion.
- I have the right to work in a safe place, where there is no bullying.
- I have the right not to be picked on.
- I have the right to speak to my teacher about something that is bothering me.
- I have the right to be listened to.

Pupils in key stages 3 and 4 took this further, and agreed a charter of rights and responsibilities in respect of racist bullying. It is shown in Table 2.1.

The principal messages from the focus groups, workshops and meetings are shown as sub-headings through the rest of this chapter.

We want you to acknowledge the complexities of racisms

Children and young people developed their own definition of racism: 'Something someone does or says that offends someone else in connection with their colour, background, culture or religion.' They broke this down further:

Racism is when:

- a person is teased or called names because of their culture or the colour of their skin, their religion, the country they come from, their language and the way they talk, the food they eat, clothes they wear or their background

- people are stereotyped by their colour or religion

- a person is rejected or excluded from a group because of their colour or religion

- people make fun of a person's family

- a person is treated unfairly because of their way of life.

It is known that one of the effects of racist bullying is that it hurts not just the target but the target's family and community. Here, significantly, making fun of a person's family was highlighted as a manifestation of racism.

Table 2.1: Charter of rights and responsibilities

We all have the right to learn in a safe, peaceful environment free from victimisation and fear. We will not tolerate any form of racist bullying, whether it is by calling people names, threatening them or hurting them in any way. We know our rights and responsibilities and we will work to protect them for ourselves and others.

I have the right	I have the responsibility
to be valued and respected for the special person I am	to value and respect others for their unique and special qualities
to work and to learn in a safe peaceful environment where I am not victimised, unhappy or afraid	to work with others to create a safe and peaceful school and to protect everyone from bullying and other forms of abuse
not to be discriminated against or bullied	not to abuse or bully others or hurt them in any way
to know how to make a complaint and where to get help	to know how to make a complaint and where to get help
to tell someone responsible if I am suffering from racist bullying, and to have my complaint listened to and dealt with	to tell someone responsible if I am suffering from racist bullying, to protect myself and other people
to tell someone responsible if I see racist bullying, or I know or think that bullying is taking place	to tell someone responsible if I see racist bullying, or I know or think that bullying is taking place, and to support others if they are suffering from racist bullying
not to be victimised if I complain of racist bullying	not to victimise anyone who makes a complaint of racist bullying

We want you to understand the causes of racism

Children and young people are impressive in their perception of the causes of racism and their attitude towards racist bullies. They look for reasons and solutions rather than blame. As causes of racism they cited:

- ignorance
- prejudice
- racist people's experiences, their history and background
- an environment where people behave in a racist way
- an environment where people's cultures and religions are not valued
- the way the people are brought up
- children and young people not having enough to do
- children and young people not succeeding in school
- peer group pressure
- having racist friends
- seeing people get away with it
- being bullied, then taking it out on someone else

These are some of the influences on people that make them racist:

- the films they see
- the magazines they read
- the TV programmes they watch
- stereotyping in the media
- racism on the street
- their peers
- their family, especially older members of the family.

With such a sophisticated understanding of the causes, it is not surprising that the solutions quoted below for preventing and dealing with racism and racist bullying are positive rather than punitive.

We want you to acknowledge that racist bullying exists

Questioned about bullying and racism, schools often assert 'there's no problem here.' Schools may make nil returns to the local authority term after term on their racist incidents reports, but is it likely that no racist comment is ever made, no name-calling ever takes place, and there is no bullying, ever? Even the best of schools, with the most cohesive community and the strongest policy and practice in pastoral matters cannot be isolated from the local and wider community. New students arrive, subject to their own influences. Pupils meet other young people in the local parks, clubs and neighbourhood. They hear opinions and learn attitudes from adults with whom they come into contact; they watch television and they read newspapers. It is highly improbable that no negative note ever creeps into school. The best schools recognise it and take continual action to combat it.

What are pupils saying about their experience of racism in school? First of all, they assert:

> We would like teachers to know that racism does happen and that teachers should confront bullies about the matter.
>
> There's bullying, and that racism happens in the classroom by notes.
>
> Teachers need to be aware that there's problems after school and at lunchtime.
>
> These examples of racism are happening in our schools and our community:
>
> - taunting children by calling them names
> - making fun of things people wear because of their religion
> - leaving people out
> - putting racist bullying in dare games
> - sending racist text messages
> - beatings up and physical violence
> - serious violence using weapons
> - setting houses alight
> - gang fights between different groups
> - taunting because of 9/11
> - taunting because of the Iraq war.

The children quoted here were particularly concerned about the amount of racist bullying in primary schools.

We want to tell you how we feel

The discussions on what happens in school that gave rise to the lists above took place in a multiethnic group aged between 5 and 18. The matter-of-fact tone contrasts sharply with statements from children and young people from minority ethnic backgrounds talking about their own experience of racism. Their statements were about their feelings. They wanted teachers to know....

how it feels to be told a racist comment and how we feel about bullying.

that racism is wrong and it affects a lot of people. It makes people upset.

The use of the word 'inside' is striking. It comes again and again.

Racists hurt the person but they don't know how much inside, so they shouldn't do it.

It's all inside me and until I come and speak to you, I don't feel better.

'They call you names for the fun of it,' wrote a nine year old boy Sikh boy quoted on the DCSF website on racist bullying, 'to make your insides weak' (DCSF, 2006:22). In a CDrom made for the Make the Difference DCSF series of anti-bullying conferences a girl who had suffered from (not racist) bullying said 'What some of the teachers don't realise is that it really, really hurts inside and you feel ... stuff ... like cutting yourself or suicide.'

The fear and stress that pupils from minority backgrounds experience is another theme running through what they are saying.

At other times, when there are parties or when some of the girls in my class are going to the pictures, I don't get invited because I am a Traveller. At break and at lunchtime, I am always looking over my shoulder because I am scared in case anyone comes up and hits me or shouts abuse at me.

These are our fears and experiences out of school

Are teachers aware of their pupils' experience of racism in day to day life outside school?

Children do not experience racism only in school – it may be an everyday occurrence outside school. It could be bullying at the hands of their schoolmates, or at the hands of strangers including adults. At worst they may not feel safe in their neighbourhood or even in their own home.

Stories in the news, added to their own experience, may contribute to a feeling of fear that they or their families might be abused or attacked. This fear may lie just under the surface, ready to rise in a moment, such as when they walk past racist graffiti, walk along a street where there have been known occurrences of racist behaviour, or recognise a racist group's dress code. Black communities have a common understanding of this fear that white communities do not share and if told, often have difficulty in accepting. After reading the book *The Life of Stephen Lawrence*, an 8 year old girl wrote:

I am also black and Stephen's story makes me feel worried that someone may act against me and I may be killed. ... I think other people who read this story will feel the same if they are black. If they are not black they should at least tell other white people who feel badly about black people that we are all the same.'

Other children and young people described their experiences and feelings out of school in these terms:

> There was one incident where people broke into my locker and wrote racist things on my books. But all of the big things happened outside school.

> There was BNP marches and language like wog and nigger being used and I got the feeling that the world doesn't want me and I don't want it either. It can get stuffed.

> Outside the school a lot of racist things happen. Some of them come from your own school and some from other schools. It's too much pressure on you. If they do something to you, you have to do something bad back to them or they won't stop.

> They put racist comments on people's doors, like 'Somali people stink'.

> They put a bonfire through your letterbox. They put lighted cigarettes as well. They throw fireworks, cigarettes, when they see you walking.

> Last time there was these bad boys upstairs on my balcony. My grandfather was walking in the street and they broke this wood and threw it at him and he had to go to hospital. The police came and the boys ran away and they ran in the bar and the police didn't get them.

> One day they broke the window on my auntie's house and hit one of my cousins. Glass went into his skin and was stuck there for about a week. He had to go to hospital. He is about 6 years old.

Treat everybody as equal

Many pupils, including those who are white British, make the specific point that African-Caribbean children are treated unfairly in school. Comments are made such as:

> At school I believe teachers teach white people more than a black person. They just believe a black person will be a troublemaker.

> More black children get kicked out of school. This can lead to crime.

Even primary school pupils understand this as racist stereotyping.

Similar comments were made in a discussion with high school pupils, and subsequently the girls prepared a paper of additional information and re-commendations. In this group it was striking that they made the connection between black boys being stereotyped in school, excluded and then getting into trouble.

Anti-Muslim racism, Islamophobia, is seen as a problem by pupils from all backgrounds. In workshops 11 September and the Iraq war were quoted as causes of racist taunting. Many of the Muslim pupils came from refugee communities. They described how they were already suppressing traumatic experiences of war and oppression.

Muslim girls in the primary school described distressingly degrading experiences in school, and terrifying experiences outside school.

> They say 'You've got nits; that's why you wear a scarf', 'Your fanny stinks'. 'Your religion hasn't got hair; that's why you wear a scarf'.

> I don't wear my hijab to school because of the bullying. I only wear it at home.

> Muslim people are scared of dogs and they chase them with dogs.

> When we go outside there's people that break windows in people's houses by throwing stones. My house – the council had to fix it. Me and other children we were in my house and they were throwing stones about three times.

Anti-Traveller racism is one of the main reasons young Travellers do not stay in school.

> They say schooldays are the best days of your life, yet I fail to see it. They could have been if it had not been for the bullies. And I know that my life could have been a lot different. If I had not been bullied, I would have been able to concentrate properly on my school work and stood a chance with my exams. I say to all the bullies out there STOP and THINK. About what you are doing, the problems you may be causing not just short term but long term. And remember how you would feel if someone did the same to you.

> I got called all sorts of names, like Gypsy, I smell, I am a tramp, I am no good, I am a pig. I had children throw stones at me, pinch me, punch me, the teacher did nothing to help me. I didn't like playtime because I knew that someone would start to bully me and that it would hurt my feelings. I always stayed near the dinner lady because they were the only ones who were a little bit nice to me.

> Source: writings collected by Gaynor Lewis and published by Cambridgeshire Race Equality and Diversity Service Team for Traveller Education, 2006.

Are you aware of the extent of racist bullying in school?

The overwhelming majority of pupils believe that teachers are not aware of the extent of racist bullying in their school.

This is mainly because bullies are crafty enough to do it away from the sight of teachers. But that is not the only reason. Pupils said that targets did not report it because they had previously tried to but the teachers had not taken effective – or, indeed, any – action. Sometimes neither targets nor bystanders report bullying because they fear reprisals. Pupils from all backgrounds complained that teachers did not believe them when they reported incidents, or did not listen, or dismissed the incident as insignificant or unimportant.

> The bullying is undercover. No one goes to staff. They say stuff about your background, skin colour and religion.

> We do not tell the teachers because they do not do anything.

> The teachers do know but they don't follow up. You get bored of telling them.

> When some people take scarves (hijab) people cuss them in the playground. Teachers don't know because they don't tell because they're scared of the teachers.

> There is bullying. If he tells the teacher the bully would punch him.

> Teachers don't listen.

> Personal comments are made at school and the students don't tell their parents or even their teacher.

Let us know where you stand

If staff are to get children and young people to report, then winning their trust is absolutely crucial. As school leavers interviewed in 2002 put it:

> You were forced into it. If you were black you were a target for racists. You are identified as a target and it comes to you. I don't know a single black person who hasn't been attacked at least verbally, and most physically. If you are a white person you can choose to be a racist at weekends and not show it during the week. It is optional whether you are involved in this stuff. It is optional whether you take it seriously.

> The teachers are mostly white. You can't look at a white person and tell if they are a racist, so if they haven't told you their views you can't go to a white person and complain about white racism.

> Most of my teachers won't have time for me. They think I am just wasting their time because all the other Travellers that have been to my school have never stuck it out as it is so lonesome.

> I don't think they know how hard it is when you are being called names every day and getting abused.

Not all teachers are unaware, and children and young people are appreciative of those who do listen and help them. There is more about this later in this chapter.

> I am Pakistani and sometimes English children are bullying me in the playground. Every time it happens the teachers get the boys.

Sometimes people bully people because they don't have the same religion. They go to the teachers but the people who did it tell fibs. At the end, the teachers tell the people who done it that they did it.

Are pupils satisfied that school staff deal adequately with racist bullying?

The young people whose views are quoted here were generally critical of the way that racist bullying was dealt with.

There's no point in telling the teachers. I've told lots of times. They did nothing. They say 'I'll find out' but there's no witness.

When I was in the juniors they used to call me names in the playground all the time, like 'nigger'. They used to upset me and sometimes I would get so mad I would fight and then I would get in trouble. I was always the one who got in trouble. They didn't do nothing to the ones that was doing it. They sent me to the head. I was crying and he told me that I mustn't fight, he said it didn't mean anything, everybody gets called names and I must rise above it. But they still kept on doing it.

Teachers always say 'Shake hands on it' but we are sorry to say that it doesn't work. The next day it happens again.

Some teachers don't listen. They don't really care. They feel it is too much bother.

Some teachers say it is telling tales.

There is unfairness to some people.

Sadly, black high school pupils interviewed had all too often given up on any hope of racist behaviour being dealt with by the school and were resigned to having to deal with it themselves. This placed them at risk of exclusion if they were not believed in the case of a consequent investigation. They were in a no-win situation.

Take measures to prevent racist bullying – educate everyone

Pupils have a clear concept of what schools should be doing. They want it to be positive and preventative rather than punitive and they urge education rather than discipline. Four principles follow from their views.

First, teachers should consult pupils on what bullying is going on in the school. It is the pupils who know. They are concerned that there should be a variety of ways of doing this, including regular discussions, setting up ways of reporting anonymously, and building up the children's confidence to speak to an adult. One practical suggestion from a group was that schools should have a named teacher who understands and whom pupils can trust for them to go to.

A second principle which goes across both preventing and addressing racist bullying is that this is an issue for the whole school community.

> Students are not told what to do about racist bullying.

> Schools should make sure everyone in school knows what they can do. Make sure that parents, teachers, caretakers, learning support assistants, cleaning staff – everybody is involved. Tell the parents to talk.

> I can recall two teachers who were approachable, kind in nature and were viewed by all pupils as a friend rather than just in a teacher/pupils relationship. They took the time to learn about diversity and different cultures and religions. They challenged the educational system and racism within the school and introduced Black History into the school curriculum. We as pupils learned about our proud history and had the guts to challenge racism in our everyday life. We had someone who we could turn to and discuss any racist incidents at school. They were role models for all teachers.

The third principle is that preventing racist bullying is a curriculum matter. The quotations here not only demonstrate what should be included in the curriculum but also that an inappropriate curriculum can actually cause racist bullying and feelings of worthlessness. Although they may not use the term, the young people certainly understand the concept of institutional racism.

> The overriding feeling was a sense of injustice at the fact that everything about the content and structure of the curriculum seemed to be saying that black people are worthless at best, never had amounted to anything and never would without the white man.

> We had Development Studies. I was taught that people in Ghana wore grass skirts and lived in mud huts until the white man came with intermediate technology.

Young people saw the broader school curriculum and teaching approaches as part of the strategy to prevent racism and bullying. They recommended that schools should:

> Spend more time to get to know more religions and cultures and learn different languages.

> Have more PSHE and RE lessons. Visit more places of worship for children to understand cultures and differences in religion. Have assemblies on different cultures and religions. Have more Circle Time.

> Do more group activities – pupils working without their chosen peers to find out about different people's backgrounds.

> Teach bullies and everyone about different races, cultures and religions. Teach people to be tolerant. Educate people everyone is equal. Train children that everyone is special.

The fourth principle in preventing racism and bullying centres on the teachers themselves:

> Teachers and school staff should have extra training, including supply teachers.

> Staff should discuss it in staff meetings.

Children feel passionately about how incidents of racism and bullying should be dealt with by schools. They should be listened to and believed:

> Listen to pupils. They *must* listen to them. They *must* give time to do this.

> Listen, even if one person is saying it happened and two people are saying they didn't do it.

> Have private meetings for people who are less confident. Give help to people who can't communicate with speech or English.

It follows that teachers should take enough time to investigate the situation thoroughly. They should be careful not to blame the wronged person instead of the bully, and once they have investigated they should make sure that the situation is dealt with:

> Teachers must take *more* time to investigate situations.

> Teachers must not punish the pupils until they get to the bottom of it. Blaming you for something you haven't done. Be careful! Be careful that bullies are not blaming the people they are bullying and telling lies about what they are doing.

> Don't label pupils as trouble makers.

> No matter how small the problem is they should take actions.

> Make sure it is dealt with.

Further, teachers should take care of the welfare of targets of bullying:

> Ask children if they're OK.

> Have a support group for people have experienced racism.

However, teachers should also make sure people who report are safe, and that those who are bullying are helped to stop:

> They *must* reassure people that their name will not be mentioned if they tell about bullying. Otherwise people will get bullied out of school.

> Reprimand children for racism in a constructive way.

Always talk to the pupils and ask them why they are picking on other pupils.

Have help for people who are racist.

Educate people who are being racist.

Sometimes people are racist without meaning to be, and teachers should help them to understand.

Give bullies and targets options to have mentors.

What do children say about their own role?

The children want to be part of the solution. Their acceptance of rights and responsibilities is a clear indication, backed up by many of the points they are making about preventing racist bullying and dealing with it when it occurs.

They ask to be kept informed about what the school is doing about racist bullying and urge the school to consult and involve them in the solution:

Give feedback in newsletters and assemblies.

Perhaps knowing how the youth feel on the topic will help broaden understanding and find an answer to this problem.

They have messages for adults, for those who are bullying, for targets of bullying and for those who witness bullying or know that it is happening. The insights, support, compassion and courage in their words to their peers are extraordinary. To the targets of bullying they say:

Don't put yourself down, *love yourself for the person you are!* Have confidence in yourself. Do not blame yourself. It is not your fault. Don't believe what the racists say and don't have low self-esteem.

Try to ignore bullies. But make sure that you do something about it. *Tell someone.* Tell your parents or guardians. Talk to a friend or a teacher or anyone else who can help you in school.

Learn about your race or religion and be proud of it.

If you're angry and feel like hitting someone, tell someone instead. You don't want to get into trouble as well.

To those who are bullying they say:

If you are being unkind to someone because of their colour or religion, that is wrong. It is called racism and it is not allowed. *Stop it!*

Everybody is equal. Always treat people how you expect to be treated. Ask yourself why you feel it necessary to bully. Try to understand how the victim is feeling.

If you need help about something, you should tell people what's bothering you. You can tell any adult in the school. Why are you bullying people? Are you bullying because you are unhappy? Are you bullying because you have problems at home? Are you bullying because of jealousy? Is anyone hurting you? Is it because you don't have friends? Have you been bullied in the past?

Do you want help to get out of bullying? You can get help. Maybe I can help you. You could talk to people. Don't be scared to tell the teachers or your friends. You can ask any adult in school who you trust for help to stop bullying.

Are you racist because you have been influenced by your family? Are you racist because of ideas you have picked up from television? You should find out more about different religions and cultures.

To those who know that racist bullying is going on, they say:

If you know someone is being unkind to someone else because of their colour or religion, that is wrong. It is called racism and it is not allowed. Don't tolerate any racist name-calling. It is bullying.

Stick up for people suffering from racism and bullying. If people are being bullied be nice to them so that no one is alone – talk to them. Help the person. Make new friends with everyone. Don't leave anyone out. Look after each other.

Tell someone. Never be scared to tell a teacher or parent or carer. If you are shy or scared, tell an adult in private. Admit that it happened. Tell someone if anyone has any problems, including yourself.

We are all equal. Everybody needs to be treated with respect. Be respectful of all cultures. Think of everybody's lifestyles and religions. Let children respect other children's beliefs by supporting their celebrations.

Tell everyone – 'Never join in with bullying or fights. Join together to say *No.*'

Concluding note

Global and national legislation and policy increasingly recommend or require the participation of children and young people. The DCSF Every Child Matters website defines this participation as:

Asking children and young people what works, what doesn't and what could work better, and involving them on an ongoing basis, in the design, delivery and evaluation of services. The Every Child Matters: Change for Children programme aims to ensure that policies and services are designed around the needs of children and young people, and that they are involved in decision making at a local and national level. Engaging children and young people in this way gives them an opportunity to make a positive contribution in their communities.

Children are indeed the experts. They must be listened to with respect. Their depth of understanding and wisdom must never be underestimated.

Throughout this book the words of young people resonate in considerations and recommendations. The next chapter considers the implications for headteachers of what we learn from them.

The last words in this chapter, urging us to take care of future generations, are from a 12 year old Somali girl:

> If teachers don't tell racists to stop, when they grow up they don't even know what they've done and the hurt that person feels, and their children get racist.

3
I need a vocabulary
Concepts, terms and distinctions

In recent years the Department for Children, School and Families (DCSF, previously Department for Education and Skills) has re-visited and expanded guidance on bullying in schools first published in the early 1990s (DfES, 1994). The more recent programme started with nine regional conferences for headteachers, with representatives from about two thousand schools altogether. At each conference there were workshops and seminars on racist bullying. At one of the first a headteacher bravely took the risk of admitting in front of his peers that he did not feel comfortable with the topic. 'I can see intuitively,' he said, 'there's a difference between racist bullying and what can be called ordinary bullying.' He continued:

> I can see there's a difference between calling someone Paki and calling someone Fatty, Ginger or Four Eyes. But what is the difference exactly? I need a vocabulary for explaining this to myself. If I cannot explain it to myself I cannot explain it to my staff. If the staff can't explain it to themselves and to each other they can't explain it to the children and we cannot explain it to parents and to the school governors. If, heaven forbid, there's a serious incident at the school, we shall not have ready answers if we are questioned by the local or national media.

There was an almost audible sigh of relief amongst the other headteachers present. Instead of trying to reduce or remove their colleague's ignorance and to showcase their own enlightenment, they acknowledged he had put his finger on a key issue – the need for action against racist bullying to be based on understandings that are conscious, explicit and rationally argued, not just intuitive. In due course, the advice published by the DfES introduced its discussion of key terms as follows (DfES, 2006a:28):

What is it we're talking about? This may seem a strange question – for everyone knows what bullying is, surely, and everyone knows what racism is, and everyone therefore knows what racist bullying is? Well, yes and no.

Yes, it's true the words bullying and racism are in widespread use and people don't turn to a dictionary to find out what they mean. But in practice people use the words in a range of ways. What one person considers bullying or racism is not necessarily what another person thinks. Discussions amongst staff can be severely hampered if the same word is used in a range of different ways.

The DfES noted in this connection that Ofsted had recommended there should be rigorous clarification in each school of the meanings of key words (Ofsted, 2003, paragraph 8):

Good school policies and training for staff analyse the different forms of bullying that pupils may experience. Unpleasant territory though it is, understanding bullying is the starting point for effective detection and response. Defining and analysing bullying can help pupils, as well as staff, to combat it.

In the light of this comment, this chapter has four sections: a) descriptions and definitions of bullying; b) descriptions and definitions of racism; c) the definition of racist bullying; and d) similarities and differences between prejudice-related bullying (including racism) and other bullying.

Descriptions and definitions of bullying

In its submission to the Select Committee on Bullying in autumn 2006, the British Psychological Society (BPS) noted there have been many academic discussions and descriptions of bullying over the years but 'as yet there is no universal agreed definition of bullying or methods to assess it' (BPS, 2006: paragraph 2.1). In consequence, since statistics depend on the operational definition being used, it is difficult or impossible to assess the general prevalence of bullying, or to compare different places and different times.

In the 1990s the focus amongst academic researchers was on physical attacks and explicit verbal abuse and they conceptualised bullying as something which essentially is perpetrated by specific individuals ('bullies' or 'perpetrators'). More recently the focus has widened to include attention also to the role of bystanders, onlookers and supporters, and therefore to the social contexts and relationships within which bullying behaviour takes place. Distinctions in this connection are drawn between *assistants* or *henchpersons*, those who join in and actively assist the ringleader(s); *reinforcers* or *bystanders*, who do not actively take part but nevertheless constitute an audience whose presence, laughter and approval encourage the ringleaders; and *outsiders*, those who shrug their shoulders and walk away, but give the ringleaders passive support by not getting involved (Ball, 2006, Coloroso, 2005). This range of roles was vividly alluded to by the children and young people quoted in chapter 2. Amongst other points, they referred to those who know that bullying is going on even though they may not themselves have witnessed it.

There is also the possibility of *defenders*, those who intervene to challenge the bullying and to give practical assistance and moral support to those who are at the receiving end. Defenders do not stand by but, as it were, stand up. Training, supporting and empowering defenders is now seen as a key element in anti-bullying strategies. The role of defenders, also known as active citizens, is particularly important in connection with prejudice-related bullying, and is highlighted later in this book (see in particular chapter 10). The roles of ringleaders, assistants, reinforcers, bystanders, outsiders and defenders are shown diagrammatically in Figure 3.1 overleaf.

Further, there has been increased attention to forms of hurtful and excluding behaviour which do not necessarily involve the use of abusive words and terms, or the use of easily identifiable actions. This form of bullying is sometimes known as relational bullying, since the purpose is to isolate someone in their relationships and render them friendless. This wider focus has been accompanied by emphasis on restorative, holistic and whole-school approaches to dealing with bullying (Hopkins, 2003; DCSF, 2007). It has also been reinforced by concerns around prejudice-related bullying (NASUWT, 2006) – not only racism (DfES, 2006) but also homophobia (DfES, 2007) and sexism (Leach and Mitchell, 2006; Womankind, 2007); by studies of the different experiences and involvements of girls and boys (Besag, 2007); and by the increasing prevalence of cyberbullying.

An extremely succinct definition of bullying was provided in a focus group discussion reported by Ofsted: 'anything that actually makes someone feel sad or uncomfortable' (Ofsted, 2008; 7). This is too general as a basis for formulating anti-bullying strategies. It does, however, valuably introduce Ofsted's essential point that 'whether something is bullying depends on how it affects the person, not on what is being done' (Ofsted, 2008.7). All bullying behaviour usually has the following four features:

1. It is repetitive and persistent – though sometimes a single incident can have precisely the same impact as persistent behaviour over time. This is because it can be experienced as part of a continuous pattern and the person at the receiving end may feel strongly that the incident is likely to be repeated. It is particularly the case with racist

Figure 3.1: BULLYING IN SCHOOLS – A DIAGRAMMATIC SUMMARY OF THE PARTS PUPILS PLAY

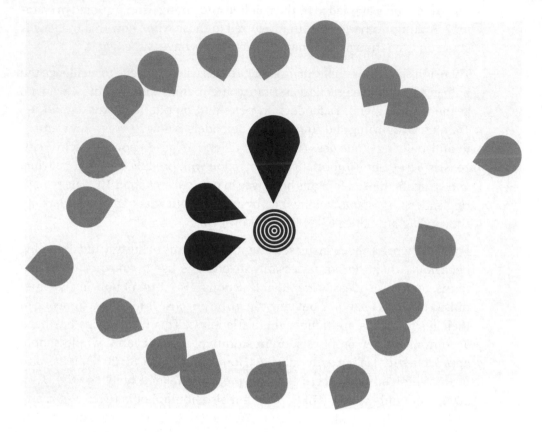

In much bullying in schools there is a range of roles that pupils may play. Most pupils take the part of bystanders – by not intervening they give the bullying their tacit approval. In the diagram above, they are shown standing around in a loose circle. In the middle of the circle there is the ringleader or chief bully, reinforced by two key supporters ('hench-persons'). Also in the middle there is the person at the receiving end of the bullying, targeted both by the ringleader and by the ringleader's two supporters. Outside the circle there are two figures. The diagram shows one who is walking away, hopefully to obtain help from a teacher. The other is coming towards the circle, hopefully to confront the bullies and to stand up for the person being targeted. Both of these are defenders or active citizens. For further discussion of the roles of bystanders and active citizens see chapter 9.

bullying, and other forms of prejudice-related bullying, that what may look like a one-off incident to a teacher is experienced as part of a pervasive climate of hostility and oppressive prejudice by the person at the receiving end.

2. It is intentionally hurtful – though occasionally the distress it causes is not consciously intended by all of those who are responsible, particularly those who are relatively passive onlookers.

3. It involves an imbalance of power, leaving someone feeling helpless to prevent it or put a stop to it. Typically though not always the imbalance is to do with numbers – ringleaders usually have assistants and an audience giving them encouragement. When there is a quarrel, disagreement or fight between two individuals or groups of equal strength this is not usually bullying.

4. It causes feelings of distress, fear, loneliness and lack of confidence in those who are at the receiving end. Such feelings can be re-activated for many years into the future, or even throughout a lifetime (Association for Psychological Science, 2008). In essence the hurt is to do with being made to feel excluded or marginalised. Sticks and stones may break my bones, to recall that famous old saying, but it can be even more devastating to feel companionless and isolated, and to feel that it is all one's own fault, and that there is nothing one can do about it.

The following points are also relevant:

■ Bullying can take many forms, including name-calling, taunting, mocking, making offensive personal comments; threatening, intimidating; creating situations in which someone is humiliated or made to look ridiculous or gets into trouble; playing tricks and pranks; spitting, kicking, hitting; pushing and jostling, and 'accidentally' bumping into someone; hiding, damaging or taking belongings; and sending malicious text messages, emails and photographs; leaving people out of groups or games or social occasions; and spreading hurtful and untrue rumours. The range of bullying behaviours does not alter the fact, to quote Ofsted again, that 'whether something is bullying depends on how it affects the person, not on what is being done'.

■ Several of these behaviours plainly involve the use of words. Several, however, equally plainly, may be non-verbal, involving body language, gesture and facial expression. To repeat, non-verbal behaviours can be just as hurtful and intimidating as those which involve abusive or threatening language.

■ A large part of the motivation behind bullying is to demonstrate power by creating fear and to gain a sense of being 'respected' by peers.

■ It often happens that young people who engage in bullying, or give it their tacit support, have themselves been bullied. Further, they may feel powerless in their current circumstances and are compensating for this by intimidating or trying to intimidate others.

■ Direct physical bullying and threats of physical bullying are more often used by boys, whereas freezing out from friendship groups is more common among girls. In recent years, however, there has been an increase in violence amongst girls.

■ Bystanders show tacit acceptance or approval and in consequence are seen by people at the receiving end as part of what they are up against.

■ Bullying within a school is sometimes directly related to, and a consequence of, tensions and feuds within and between groups, families and communities in the local neighbourhood.

Descriptions and definitions of racism

Most public bodies in the UK use the working definitions of racism and racist incident that were proposed in the report of the Stephen Lawrence Inquiry, 1999. The report defined racism as 'conduct or words or practices which disadvantage or advantage people because of their colour, culture or ethnic origin' (Macpherson, 1999, paragraph 6.4) and commented that 'in its more subtle form it is as damaging as in its overt form'. It recommended that a racist incident should be defined as 'any incident which is perceived to be racist by the victim or any other person' (Macpherson, 1999: recommendation 12). The report valuably stressed that racism is expressed through customs, practices and procedures as well as through one-off actions and words; that it provides advantages and privileges to some people at the same time as inflicting disadvantages on others; and that key markers of supposedly significant difference are to do not only with physical appearance ('colour') but also with culture and ethnicity.

There is a single human race. Terms such as *racial group*, *race equality* and *race relations* are therefore always in danger of being misleading, particularly when they are enshrined in legislation. The term *race* does, however, invaluably allude to racism. The United Nations World Conference Against Racism (WCAR) in 2001 summarised its concerns with the phrase 'racism, racial discrimination, xenophobia and related intolerance'. The equivalent phrase used by the Council of Europe is 'racism, xenophobia, antisemitism and intolerance'. The definition of racism used by the European Commission against Racism and Intolerance (ECRI) is: '... the belief that a ground such as 'race', colour, language, religion, nationality or national or ethnic origin justifies contempt for a person or a group of persons, or the notion of superiority of a person or group of persons' (ECRI, 2002: paragraph 1.1).

ECRI's references to religion, language and nationality are a reminder that in nearly every kind of racism there is both a biological and a cultural strand. The strands appear in different combinations at different times, however, and in different places. The biological strand uses physical features of perceived difference, particularly skin colour and facial features, to recognise 'the other'. The cultural strand refers to differences of religion, language and way of life. Both strands involve believing that certain differences amongst human beings are fixed as well as significant, can justify unjust distributions of power and resources, and can determine who is and who is not a full or real member of the national society. The distinction is sometimes said to be between colour racism and cultural racism, or between North-South racism and West-East racism. Such phrases have their uses, but obscure the reality that physical and cultural markers are usually combined. (Commission on the Future of Multi-Ethnic Britain, 2000:56-66).

The plural term 'racisms' is sometimes used to highlight such complexity. For anti-black racism is different from anti-Asian racism in terms of its historical and economic origins and in its contemporary manifestations, stereotypes and effects. Both are different from, to cite three further significant examples, anti-Irish, anti-Gypsy and anti-Jewish racism. European societies, it is sometimes said, are multi-racist societies. Specific words have been coined over the years for certain types of racism directed at particular groups – the term antisemitism originated in the mid nineteenth century, and more recently the terms orientalism and Islamophobia have been coined to refer to anti-Asian racism in general and to anti-Muslim racism in particular.

Latterly, a set of phenomena has emerged in western Europe that is known as anti-refugee racism or xeno-racism (Sivanandan, 2001). Xeno-racism is directed at 'those who, displaced and dispossessed by globalisation, are being thrown up on Europe's shores' (Kundnani, 2006). It receives its energy and support from the millions of white Europeans who also are displaced and dis-possessed by, amongst other things, global forces over which they have no control. Their employment prospects are threatened and so is the sense of cultural and national identity with which they grew up.

Defining racist bullying

On the basis of the discussions above of bullying and racism, racist bullying can be defined as:

> a range of hurtful behaviour, both physical and psychological, that makes a person feel unwelcome, marginalised, excluded, powerless or worthless because of their colour, ethnicity, culture, faith community, national origin or national status. (DfES, 2006a:33)

This is the definition of racist bullying used throughout this book. The term prejudice-related bullying refers more widely to bullying that is connected with prejudices around belonging, identity and equality in wider society, in particular prejudices to do with disabilities and special educational needs; gender; home life, for example in relation to issues of care, parental occu-pation, poverty and social class; and sexuality.

It is relevant to note that all instances of racist bullying in schools are racist incidents, as defined by the Stephen Lawrence Inquiry report. However, not all racist incidents are necessarily instances of racist bullying. This is because not all have the features of bullying outlined earlier in this chapter. For example, if two pupils have an argument in the playground, and if in the heat of the moment the one uses a derogatory term about the other's cultural or ethnic background, this would be recorded as a racist incident; it would pro-bably not, however, be thought of as an example of bullying. Or if a pupil uses inappropriate language in a classroom discussion this too might be recorded as a racist incident, but would not be thought of as an example of bullying.

Similarities and differences

The headteacher quoted at the start posed a crucial question: what is the dif-ference between racist bullying on the one hand and what he called ordinary bullying on the other? In certain ways, however, it was not the most pressing question to ask first. The beginning of wisdom in the present context lies in identifying similarities. These may be itemised as follows:

- ■ Pupils at the receiving end experience great distress. They may be-come fearful, depressed and lacking in self-confidence, and reluctant to attend school. Their progress at school may be severely damaged.

Their distress is connected with feelings of being left out, excluded and rejected. Also, the distress arises because one of their characteristics is often picked out as a justification for the bullying they can do nothing about – their size, wearing glasses, the colour of their hair, the colour of their skin, their gender, an impairment, their religious or cultural background. Since all kinds of bullying cause distress, all are wrong. There is no hierarchy of bullying.

■ Teachers and even parents are sometimes unaware of the miseries that are being inflicted or the cruelty that is being perpetrated.

■ The same range of methods of bullying is used – verbal abuse and name-calling, physical attacks and threats, spreading rumours, excluding from friendship groups, and leaving pernicious messages on mobile phones and web spaces. However, girls and boys engage in bullying in different ways.

■ When dealing with incidents, staff must attend to a) the needs, feelings and wishes of pupils at the receiving end, b) the needs, feelings and wishes of their parents and carers, c) the children and young people principally responsible for the bullying, d) any supporters they have, e) any bystanders and witnesses and f) the school community as a whole. There is an important potential role for restorative and holistic approaches in place of an emphasis on sanctions and punishment.

Within the context of these similarities, colour-blind and culture-blind approaches to dealing with bullying do not work. By the same token, 'difference-blind' approaches do not work in relation to other forms of prejudice-related bullying. The following points must be borne in mind.

■ Prejudices have a long history affecting millions of people and are a common feature in wider society. People are seriously harmed and injured by them, and sometimes even viciously attacked and murdered. Words such Spotty, Ginger, Fatty and Four Eyes are seldom used by adults and seldom if ever used by adults to justify offensive behaviour. Forms of prejudice-related bullying, however, are associated with discrimination in employment and the provision of services, and with a range of criminal offences. It follows that children do not necessarily 'grow out of' them.

■ There is tacit or even explicit support for certain prejudices in the conservative press, radio phone-in programmes and some television. In particular there is support for prejudices against Muslim people,

Travellers and Gypsies, people seeking asylum, and people who are gay, lesbian or bisexual.

■ The law of the land recognises the seriousness of racist and religious prejudice by requiring that courts should impose higher sentences when an offence is aggravated by racist or religious hostility. Similar developments in the criminal justice system are likely in relation to other kinds of prejudice-related incident.

■ Racist bullying is in principle a criminal offence and can lead to a pupil acquiring a criminal record.

■ The distinctive feature of a prejudice-related attack or insult is that a person is attacked or insulted not as an individual, as in most other offences, but as the representative of a family, community or group. Other members of the same group, family or community are in consequence made to feel threatened and intimidated as well. So it is not just the pupil who is attacked who feels unwelcome or marginalised. 'When they call me a Paki,' explains 9-year-old Sereena, 'it's not just me they're hurting. It's all my family and all other black people too' (quoted in DfES, 2006).

■ Or for example all women are intimidated if a single woman is attacked in a lonely place; all disabled people feel threatened and reluctant to go out into public spaces when they hear of an attack on a single disabled individual; all gay, lesbian and bisexual people have their liberty of movement curtailed by an attack on an individual who is believed to be not heterosexual.

■ Prejudice-related words and behaviour are experienced as attacks on the values, loyalties and commitments central to a person's sense of identity and self-worth. Often, therefore, they hurt not only more widely but also more deeply. 'They attack me for being an Arab', remarks Ahmed. 'But I'm an Arab because my father is an Arab, and I love my father. Do they think I should stop loving my father? I couldn't do that, ever' (quoted in DfES, 2006).

■ A message in all bullying is 'you don't belong'. In the case of racist bullying the message is not only 'you don't belong in this playground or this friendship group' but also 'you don't belong in this country'; it is often, therefore, even more devastating and traumatic than other forms of bullying for the pupil who is attacked.

■ Prejudice-related attacks are committed not only against a community but also, in the eyes of offenders themselves, on behalf of a community – they see themselves as representative of, and supported in their behaviour by, their friends, family and peer group, and they may well feel it is right and proper to take the law into their own hands.

■ Quite apart from whether those responsible see themselves as representatives of their own community taking the law into their own hands, this is how they may be seen by those at the receiving end. So a disabled child, for example, may come to fear and distrust all non-disabled people, not just those who bully.

Concluding note

Much discourse about bullying and racist incidents in schools refers to 'perpetrators' and 'victims'. This chapter has argued that the first of these terms is unsatisfactory as it implies the focus should only or mainly be on individuals rather than also on the social situation in which bullying takes place and the role of henchpersons and bystanders.

The term victim is apposite in so far as it implies that people at the receiving end of bullying are not themselves in any way to blame. Like victims of road accidents or natural disasters they are in the wrong place at the wrong time. The word victim implies further that intervention is required from others. The word is misleading, however, in so far as it may lead to a victim mentality, a sense of learned helplessness. Even more seriously, it may be depersonalising and reductionist, ignoring the individuality, interests, needs, strengths and wishes of a unique human being, with a unique history and a unique future, who is at the moment in a unique situation with unique desires and needs (Kaufman *et al*, 1999; Alexander, 2003; Lovegrove, 2006).

In 2004 the DfES organised a poetry competition for children on the theme of bullying in schools. The prize-winning entries were said by the poet Andrew Fusek Peters (Peters, 2005:1) to be expressing and communicating this essential message: 'Listen to me. I am here. I am worth something. I am more than just a victim.'

The headteacher quoted at the start of this chapter will hopefully find this chapter helpful, if he happens to read it, and will be pleased that his brave question generated so much useful deliberation in the years that followed. He may take appropriate pride in having started an invaluable debate and process of clarification. Hopefully he will also find the next chapter helpful. It is about four broad approaches to dealing with incidents: the dismissive, the punitive, the corrective and the transformative. The fourth involves seeing and attending to the worth of everyone. Everyone is here, is worth something, is more than just a victim.

RESPONDING

4

Oh, just call them something back
Dealing and not dealing with incidents

'We were bussed to a faraway school,' recalls the journalist Amila Baig looking back to her childhood in the 1980s (Baig, 2007), 'where we were the only children with brown faces. When we got called names the teachers would say: 'Oh just call them something back like milky."

'Some insult,' comments Baig. 'The Milky Bar Kid was strong and tough.' She was a feisty young person, it can readily be imagined: her objection to the advice she received from teachers was not that their whole approach was wrongheaded but that they did not arm her with a fiercer, more cutting insult than 'milky' with which to take on her tormentors. The teachers' concern to help her stand up for herself had its positive aspects – at least they did not encourage her to see herself as a helpless victim. Their failure to take seriously what she was telling them, however, not only about her own experiences but also about the attitudes and behaviour of other children, and about the ethos of the school as a whole, was outrageous. But what *should* they have done? How could they and how should they have prevented episodes such as this occurring? These are the fundamental questions of this chapter. It distinguishes between four broad approaches to dealing with racist incidents and bullying in schools and names these as a) dismissive b) punitive c) corrective and d) transformative. It is particularly concerned with describing and commending the fourth approach.

In broad terms though not in its specific words, this fourfold typology was developed on the basis of research commissioned in the 1990s by the Racist Attacks Group based at the Home Office (Sibbitt, 1997). The focus in the first instance was on street racism as distinct from playground racism, so included adults as well as children. Its purpose, however, was entirely relevant to schools: 'to comment on what approaches are likely to be most effective in tackling racial harassment by interventions with those responsible and preventative work with potential perpetrators' (Sibbitt, 1997:vii). The research methodology was qualitative: evidence was collected from case studies in two London boroughs and interviews were held with police officers, probation officers, youth workers, housing officials and teachers, and people directly involved in racist violence as offenders or at the receiving end. The main findings included:

- People responsible for racist harassment and violence on the streets include children and young people as well as adults of all ages, including pensioners. They are both male and female and often act together as groups of friends or as families. Some are involved also in other kinds of anti-social and criminal behaviour.

- Their views are shared by the wider communities to which they belong and they see this as legitimising their behaviour.

- Racist actions and expressions of racist attitudes often function to distract people's attention away from underlying concerns which they feel impotent to deal with. Such concerns include a sense of dispossession, marginalisation and lack of identity, insecurity about the future and physical or mental health problems.

- Action to prevent racist violence must accordingly include work not only with those who are directly responsible but also those who are potential offenders and those who are members of the supportive climate of opinion ('the perpetrator community') within which those responsible live and move, and whose approval they take for granted. Further, it must tackle delinquency and criminality in general, not racist offences in particular, and must address underlying causes connected with stress, insecurity, territory and identity, as distinct from 'adopting a simplistic approach based on moral opprobrium' (Sibbitt, 1997:viii).

- In brief, action to prevent racist violence and harassment on the streets must ideally include: a) removing factors which are conducive to stress, delinquency and criminality and b) removing factors likely to generate racist prejudice and hostility towards 'the other'.

These findings were subsequently confirmed by a literature review conducted for the Runnymede Trust by Omar Khan (2002). Sibbitt's research concluded that there are four principal ways in which teachers, youth workers and other professionals may react to an individual's expressions of racism. It summarised these (Sibbitt, 1997:104) as:

- not responding at all
- responding with moral opprobrium
- directly attempting to deconstruct racist arguments
- addressing racist attitudes in the context of a more holistic approach.

There are brief notes on each of these below, adapting them to school contexts and using different key words.

Approach 1: Dismissive

Ignoring or making light of an incident, in the way Anila Baig's teachers did, is seldom if ever appropriate. It permits the person responsible for the bullying – and also friends and associates, and any witnesses and bystanders – to assume there's nothing wrong with their behaviour. The behaviour may therefore be repeated.

More seriously, this approach gives no support to the pupils at the receiving end. They may in consequence assume teachers and the school are indifferent to the prejudice and hostility in the school and in society, and will see no point in complaining if further incidents occur, as was vividly illustrated in chapter 2. They may feel that the school does not care for them, does not understand their experiences and perceptions, does not see them as fully belonging. Feelings of being excluded and worthless, caused by the bullying, will be exacerbated. This is what appears to have happened to Anila Baig: a picture builds up of the whole school being insensitive and uncaring. In the same breath in which she recalls how teachers failed to respond to racist name-calling, Baig recalls insensitivity at the hands of a lunchtime assistant (Baig, 2007):

> At lunchtime, we had to finish up whatever was on our plates, whether it was chicken pie or pork sausages. I was asked if I was a vegetarian but I didn't know what that was. 'Do you eat meat?' the dinner lady enunciated loudly. Well, yes I did at home. 'Eat it up then, chop chop.'

Baig also links the insensitivity of staff at the school she attended with violent racism on the streets and with crude stereotypes in TV programmes such as *Till Death Us Do Part*:

> Racism was in-yer-face – along with a fist if you were really unlucky. Television programmes featured lovable racist characters and it was a bit of a laugh.

Approach 2: Punitive

Pupils responsible for bullying – and any onlookers – must be in no doubt that their behaviour is unacceptable, and those at the receiving end of bullying must be in no doubt they are supported by their school. But if disapproval is expressed and punishments are meted out but not complemented by teaching and learning about why bullying is wrong and why prejudice-related bullying in particular is wrong, the sanctions may feed bitterness and a sense of not being understood. Such bitterness may then be expressed elsewhere, unknown to the school.

This approach, writes Sibbitt (1997:104)

> ... effectively silences the individual when in the presence of the professional, but is likely to have limited impact on his or her expression of such attitudes more generally... The opportunity to address these attitudes constructively has been lost, and future opportunities, where the individual meets with other professions and fails to speak openly, may also have been undermined.'

It may well happen that young people learn to live double lives – apparently not racist when in the presence or hearing of teachers, but contentedly and defiantly racist in their attitudes when with their family and friends. Zero tolerance, remarks Barbara Coloroso, can equal zero-thinking. (Coloroso, 2005:204-7)

Approach 3: Corrective

'I just tell the children racism is against the law, end of story,' said someone at one of the teacher workshops that led eventually to DfES guidance for schools on dealing with racist incidents (DfES, 2006). 'I fill in a form when an incident occurs and that's that, problem sorted.' In the hectic day-to-day life of schools and classrooms, with its plethora of pressures and events demanding attention, it is inevitable that not every moment will be a teachable moment, an opportunity to correct rather than to control. Sometimes control takes priority over helping someone to learn. Teachers are first and foremost educators not police officers. Their professional responsibility is to help children learn and understand for themselves why some actions are wrong and others right. Racism is not wrong because the law says so; rather, the law says so because racism is wrong.

It is important, therefore, that teachers and youth workers should explain why prejudice is wrong, and that they should demonstrate with facts, statistics and rational arguments that prejudiced beliefs and behaviours are false and harmful. This is likely to involve deconstructing specific lines of thought, pointing out contradictions and inconsistencies, and showing that even when a factual statement is true ('They own all the corner shops round here') it does not logically justify harassment, abuse or violence. Also, it is likely to involve challenging over-generalisations and will almost certainly involve explaining why prejudiced-related bullying is distinctively hurtful.

But like expressions of disapproval and punishments, intellectual arguments may feed bitterness and a sense of not being understood. Pupils may also feel an increased sense of personal inferiority and powerlessness, and greater resentment of authority, and may become even more prejudiced in their attitudes and behaviour. This might attract them to claims by organisations such as the British National Party and journalists in the conservative press that the country is being destroyed by 'the political correctness brigade' and by something called multiculturalism (see chapter 1). 'It is important,' remark researchers based at the Institute for Public Policy Research, 'not to assume that misunderstanding or lack of knowledge is solely at the root of hostile attitudes, or that increasing people's knowledge will increase tolerance. Some people simply are not motivated to know more and when this is the case shifting attitudes through information provision becomes impossible' (Lewis and Newman, 2007:23).

Sibbitt comments:

> Clearly the task for the professional ... is firstly to gain the trust and respect of the individual by recognising their needs and, as far as possible, helping the individual either to meet those needs or to live with them. During this period of confidence-building, the professional will need to avoid appearing to connive, however passively, in the individual's hostility towards minorities, and they may actively assert their own values. However, it may be only once the necessary trust and respect have been earned that they can ... constructively address these attitudes. (Sibbitt, 1997:105)

Approach 4: restorative and transformative

On the basis of her criticisms of the first three approaches Sibbitt proposes what she calls a holistic approach. More recently, theorists have termed this restorative or transformative rather than holistic. The primary objectives of a restorative approach (Marshall, 1999) are to:

- attend fully to the emotional and social needs of those who are at the receiving end of bullying and those who are close to them

- prevent re-offending by enabling offenders to assume active responsibility for their actions and reintegrating them into the school community

- avoid escalation, and mounting expense of time and energy
- repair and recreate the community that has been damaged by the bullying, with a view to making it more active in preventing further bullying in the future.

Belinda Hopkins (2003:18-19) itemises the advantages and benefits of restorative approaches to bullying in schools as follows. For those at the receiving end, there are opportunities to:

- be given information about what is happening in their case
- have someone listen sympathetically to their experience
- have questions answered about why the offence occurred (for example, 'why me?')
- tell those responsible how they have been affected
- ask those responsible for compensation or reparation of some sort
- receive an apology and see that the offender is genuinely remorseful
- help the offender
- meet the offender in a situation where they are not helpless.

For those who are responsible for bullying, the benefits of a restorative approach include opportunities to:

- acknowledge responsibility and face up to what they have done by hearing and acknowledging the harm they have caused, not only directly to those at the receiving end but also, indirectly, to the fabric of the school community
- see and show themselves in a better light by answering questions, being reflective, apologising, and doing things to make amends.

Howard Zehr (2002) stresses that the essential purpose of the restorative approach is to put right the wrongs and harms that have been caused. It does this by:

- focusing on the harms and consequent needs of those at the receiving end, as well as the harms and needs of the community and of offenders
- addressing the obligations that arise from those harms, particularly the obligations of the offender and the wider community

■ using inclusive, collaborative processes

■ involving all stakeholders, including not only those at the receiving end and those responsible but also parents and friends, audiences and bystanders, and the wider community.

'Underlying restorative justice,' Zehr says (2002:35), 'is the vision of inter-connectedness ... We are all connected to each other and to the larger world through a web of relationships. When this web is disrupted, we are all affected. The primary elements of restorative justice – harm and need, obligation and participation – derive from this vision.' He continues:

> But this value of interconnectedness must be balanced by an appreciation for particularity. Although we are connected, we are not the same. Particularity appreciates diversity. It respects the individuality and worth of each person. It takes seriously specific context and situations. Justice must acknowledge both our interconnections and our individuality. The value of particularity reminds us that context, culture and personality are all important.

In sum, Zehr's definition of restorative justice (page 37) is 'a process to involve, to the extent possible, those who have a stake in a specific offence and to collectively identify and address harms, needs and obligations, in order to heal and put things as right as possible.' He acknowledges that restorative justice, as distinct from punitive justice, is often a counsel of perfection and impracticable. To contrast it with punitive justice, however, is to draw attention to views and questions that might otherwise not get a sufficient hearing. Table 4.1 outlines the key differences.

Table 4.1: Differences between punitive justice and restorative justice

Key questions	Punitive justice	Restorative justice
What is crime?	A violation of the law and the state	Crime is a violation of people and relationships
What do violations create?	Guilt	Needs and obligations
What should be the central focus?	Offenders getting what they deserve	The needs of those who have been hurt and the obligations of offenders to repair harm
What does justice require?	That those who are guilty should be identified and punished.	That victims, offenders and the community work together to put things right

Source: adapted slightly from Zehr (2002)

Key points in a restorative approach to dealing with racist bullying and incidents include the following.

- Children's prejudiced beliefs and behaviour are driven by anxieties about identity and territory, and desires to belong to a sub-culture of peers or a gang where racism, sexism and homophobia are some (though usually not all) of the principal features.

- Those who are responsible, it follows, often operate as a group rather than as single individuals, and teachers need to engage not only with those most obviously responsible but also with witnesses, by-standers, audiences and supporters.

- Teachers and youth workers should show they understand the anxieties and desires children have around identity, belonging and self-esteem, and do their best to engage with them.

- The anxieties and attitudes expressed in prejudice-related behaviour and bullying among young people are frequently expressed or tacitly encouraged in the print media, for example in relation to Muslims, migrant workers and people seeking asylum, and in media discussions of so-called political correctness.

- All pupils should be involved in dealing with prejudice-related incidents, for example through peer mediation activities. It is not just a matter for adults.

- Teachers need to have a shared personal and professional philosophy about the nature of diverse society and how to deal with conflicts, controversies and difference in such a society.

- Attention should be paid to preventing and reducing prejudice-related bullying through the curriculum (particularly but by no means only the citizenship and PSHE curriculum) and in the overall ethos of the school.

Restorative justice, particularly in the context of this book's concern with racist incidents and bullying in schools, might be criticised as not being ambitious enough. The task should be not merely to 'restore' the *status quo* but to transform it. The argument that the concept of 'transformative justice' is more dynamic and fruitful than mere restoration has been made by, amongst others, Canadian theorist and activist John Paul Lederach (for example, Lederach, 2003) and Norwegian peace campaigner Johan Galtung (for example, Galtung, 2004). Whether Lederach and Galtung are right at the level

Box 4.1: Things that happen

Used to it

Someone of Sri Lankan background has recently taken over a local shop. He mentions in conversation with a teacher that he gets a lot of low-level racist abuse from certain pupils at the school. He's used to it, he says, and doesn't want to make a formal complaint.

Doesn't appear to mind

A girl from Poland has recently joined the class. She is addressed as Pollywog by a group of other girls and doesn't appear to mind.

Playing football

Boys playing football in the playground are heard calling each other Nigger and Paki.

Retaliates

Geoffrey, who is of Traveller heritage, has annoyed Darren. Darren retaliates angrily, and calls him Pikey.

My dad agrees

In an RE lesson a pupil produces a leaflet published by the British National Party.

'We owe it to our children to defend our Christian culture,' it says. And: 'Are you concerned about the growth of Islam in Britain?' The pupil says: 'My dad agrees with this. Do you, miss?'

White bitch

Pupils are queuing up in the canteen at lunchtime waiting. There's some pushing and shoving and a girl is pushed into another girl, knocking her tray out of her hands. The girl whose tray has been knocked turns to the other girl and calls her a white bitch.

I feel they don't like me

'No-one's ever called me a nasty name,' a pupil tells a teacher, 'but all the same I feel the other girls don't like me, and I think they're spreading rumours about me. I think it's because of my colour.'

Same as most teachers

'You only ever pick on black or Asian kids,' says a pupil to a teacher. 'You're racist, that's why, same as most white people.'

Source: adapted from material at (www.teachernet.gov.uk/racistbullying)

of semantics is far less important than that the principles and precepts underlying the concept of conflict transformation are relevant to dealing with racist incidents in schools. The concept does not negate or contradict Sibbitt's emphasis on holism or Hopkins' and Zehr's emphasis on restoration of relationships, but can extend and enrich them.

Concluding note

In staff training sessions the four approaches can valuably be compared and contrasted through discussion of real or imagined events. Box 4.1 shows the kind of event that can be considered. In each instance it is relevant to discuss a) what should be done in the next five minutes b) what should be done in the next five hours and c) what should be done in the next five weeks. A transformative approach might well involve also considering what should be done in the next five years.

The dismissive approach adopted by Anila Baig's teachers was clearly inadequate. The logic of the restorative and transformative approaches described and commended in this chapter is that there needs to be attention to the whole curriculum in schools and to whole-school issues relating to leadership, organisation and staff training. Chapters 6-12 of this book deal with such matters. The next chapter discusses processes of recording and reporting. This may seem rather mechanistic in light of the need for transformation outlined above. However, governing bodies of schools in the UK are required by law to report racist incidents to their local authorities, and authorities for their part are expected to publish periodic reports. The requirement to report is sometimes experienced by teachers and officers as a tiresome bureaucratic chore. But it has the potential to be an integral part of the process argued for in this chapter: transformation.

5

Racist incidents in schools at new high
Recording and reporting, problems and potential

The headline facts appear at first sight clear. 'Racist incidents in schools at new high,' says a local paper based in east London (Campbell, 2008) and 'Racist incidents rise in south Bucks schools,' says a Buckinghamshire paper a few weeks later (Evans, 2008). Headlines in local newspapers published between these two, however, include 'Warwickshire schools see drop in racist incidents' (Lynch, 2008), reporting that 'the number of racist incidents ... has fallen dramatically after several years on the rise', and 'Racist incidents in schools are falling', about schools in South Tyneside. Are there different trends in different parts of the country? Or are there differences in how racist incidents in schools are recorded and reported at different times and in different places? Either way, how could and should systems of recording and reporting be improved? Should they be standardised across England or even across the whole of the UK? If so, how? How can recording and reporting incidents be genuinely valuable, instead of just a bureaucratic chore? These are the principal questions explored in this chapter.

Much the same questions are raised by an item in the single equality scheme of the Qualifications and Curriculum Authority (QCA, 2007:23):

> The number of racist incidents recorded in Leeds schools jumped from 1,142 in 2002/3 to 1,430 in 2005/6. Over the same period Birmingham schools saw an increase from 832 to 1,577, and Manchester schools rose from 590 to 696. Other noticeable rises in racist reports occurred in Bolton, Coventry, Derby, Dudley, Kent and Lancashire.

The QCA's figures were quoted from a survey carried out earlier in 2007 by Channel Four News (Hannam, 2007). A freedom of information probe of more than 90 education authorities in England had, according to Channel Four itself, 'exposed the true extent of racist tensions in schools', with nearly 100,000 incidents documented over the previous four years. Cities such as Leeds, Manchester and Birmingham, said Channel Four, had 'seen a distinct hike in reported racism in the classroom'. In point of fact, none of these cities had provided data about incidents in classrooms as distinct from other spaces in and around schools. This kind of careless reporting in the media does nothing to foster informed deliberation and decision-making in schools and local authorities. However, this is a small point compared with the overall situation to which Channel Four was drawing attention. Similarly it is insignificant compared with the fact that in 2004-05, the most recent year for which data was available when a parliamentary question was asked by Lorely Burt MP on 26 April 2007, there were 40 permanent and 3,390 fixed period exclusions from English schools for racist abuse. These figures compared with 130 permanent and 7,680 fixed period exclusions for all types of bullying.

All the figures cited above are from local authority reports, based on statistical returns from schools. In addition there are facts and figures collected directly from pupils, for individual schools and local authorities sometimes include questions about racist bullying in surveys of pupils' experiences and opinions. One of the most substantial studies yet undertaken in this respect took place in Hampshire in 2005. It involved a sample of 34,428 pupils and was part of a programme of surveys begun in 2000. In 2005, in consultation with headteachers, the authority added questions about experiences of bullying, including racist bullying. It was found that almost a fifth (19%) of Year 9 pupils had experienced bullying at school in the previous 12 months; in Years 6 and 7 the proportion was about a quarter (23% and 25% respectively) and in Year 2 it was more than a third (37%).

For the question about bullying around racism, culture and religion, pupils in Year 2 were asked to tick Yes or No in response to a statement that was read to them: 'Since I have been in year 2 someone has been unkind to me in school or in the playground because of the colour of my skin or my religion, or because the language I speak at home is not English.' For older pupils the question required Yes or No in reply to a similar statement in writing: 'In the last year, I have been picked on in school because of my skin colour or religion or because the language I speak at home is not English.' It could be estimated from the pattern of answers that in all four year groups virtually every single pupil of a minority heritage in the sample answered Yes. It is relevant to recall the young person quoted at the start of chapter 2: 'I don't know a single black person who hasn't been attacked at least verbally, and most physically'.

Such surveys are valuable for raising awareness of the prevalence of racist bullying and providing a framework for more open discussion and hopefully more effective action, than would otherwise occur. In the case of Hampshire the data is given to school improvement partners (SIPs) and used in assessments of how effectively schools are meeting the five Every Child Matters outcomes. The data is also used to assess the implementation of race equality policies and the authority's race equality scheme, and discussion and action are linked to Hampshire's programme for human rights education.

Research sponsored by the DfES in mainly white schools in 2001/02 found that 25 per cent of the pupils from minority backgrounds in the sample had experienced racist name-calling within the past seven days. In interviews undertaken as part of the same research, a third of the pupils of minority ethnic backgrounds reported experiences of hurtful name-calling and verbal abuse either at school or during the school journey, and for about a half of these (one in six overall) the harassment was continuing or had continued over an extended period of time (Cline *et al*, 2002). Several years later research funded by the Economic and Social Research Council confirmed there are severe problems of prejudice in mainly white schools (Brown, 2008 and see also Gaine, 2005 and Troyna and Hatcher, 1992).

A guidance paper issued by the DfES in December 2006 had the potential to bring some standardisation across different local authorities but unfortunately this was not achieved or even explicitly intended. Nor was there a reference to standardisation in an Ofsted thematic report published in autumn 2005. This merely observed that it is up to local authorities to decide with their schools what constitutes a racist incident, and that good practice in this respect means 'liaison with other partners, such as the police, to ensure that each agency in the local authority's area has a settled, common definition of what represents a race-related incident'. Local consultation and liaison are important and valuable, but it is unsatisfactory to disregard the complexities of trying to integrate the broadly punitive remit of the police with the educative remit of schools, or the complexities of 150 local authorities in England each negotiating on its own with one of 43 police authorities.

It is not known what degree of standardisation already exists in England. Research in Scotland, however, has shown that each of 32 education authorities pursues its own approach to recording racist incidents in schools (York Consulting, 2006: paragraph 6.5) and that the majority (23 out of 32) do not provide any rationale for recording and monitoring racist incidents – 'occasionally information is provided about the race relations legislation but generally the guidance launches straight into a definition of a racist incident and the detail of how to record and complete the monitoring forms' (paragraph 4.10), with no explanation of the purpose and possible benefits. The fundamental conclusion from the research is that 'a set of good practice national guidance should be produced that addresses the gaps and divergence within existing policies and offers a coherent and supportive set of materials' (paragraph 6.26). A similar development is required for England and for Wales.

A major problem with the current system in many local authorities is the under-reporting of racist incidents. Commenting on the Channel Four data mentioned above, Heidi Mirza, director of the Centre for Rights, Equalities and Social Justice at the University of London Institute of Education, observed that the statistics were 'just the tip of the iceberg. There are a lot of young people who don't want to report this because they are too embarrassed or frightened to do so. I think there's a definite problem with racism in schools, I think one of the biggest issues we have is actually the under-reporting of these incidents (Mirza, 2007)'. A further problem is that there is, in most published reporting, no indication of the seriousness of incidents – there is seldom more detail than the distinction between 'physical' and 'verbal'. Connected with this is a simplistic notion that racist bullying is little more than a relationship between a 'perpetrator' and a 'victim', and the fact that invisible actions – freezing someone out of a friendship group, for example, or spreading false rumours – do not get recorded, even though they may be more hurtful than a racist word spoken in the heat of a quarrel.

The legal expectation, following the Stephen Lawrence Inquiry (Macpherson, 1999, recommendation no.68) is that schools will report to their local authority the number of racist incidents involving members of the school community at or near their premises each year, and that the local authorities will each year compile an aggregated report of the kind that led to the headlines cited at the start of this chapter, and to the data summarised by Channel Four. Until April 2008 the Audit Commission's best value performance indicators (BVPIs) required local authorities to report the numbers of racist incidents per 100,000 residents (BVPI 174) and the numbers of incidents in which follow-up action was taken (BVPI 175). This involved aggregating all incidents in schools with all incidents in other local authority services and departments and produced totals that were of no conceivable practical use. Since April 2008 the requirement has no longer been in force.

The legal, inspection and auditing requirements following the Stephen Lawrence Inquiry led to increased attention to racist incidents in schools and how to deal with them, and this has been for the good. For example, a number of authorities now provide a substantial rationale for recording and reporting. One way of doing this is through answers to frequently asked questions. The material below is adapted from a local authority which adopted this approach (Ealing, 2003) and from the DfES (DfES, 2006a:47-50).

Frequently asked questions

Why does the definition of racist incidents stress perception? Procedures in schools should be based on objective tests and evidence, surely, not on subjective impressions and perceptions?

- The definition of racist incident was drafted in the first instance by the Association of Chief Police Officers (ACPO) and then modified slightly by the Stephen Lawrence Inquiry (Macpherson, 1999). ACPO was concerned that too many incidents were not even being recorded properly, let alone professionally and rigorously investigated.

- The definition implies that if anyone thinks an incident is racist then it will definitely be taken seriously and investigated. Failure to investigate, even where an incident appears to be of a relatively minor nature, could be seen as condoning racism and could be used as evidence that a school is not taking seriously its legal duties under the Race Relations Act, as amended.

- Whether or not the pupils responsible intended their behaviour to be racist is in the first instance irrelevant, although when it comes to dealing with an incident, pupils' intentions and attitudes require consideration. But at the stage of initial recording and investigating, their attitudes, motivation and awareness are not the main issue. It's the effects of their behaviour, not the reasons for it, that require attention.

Should schools aim for a nil return to the local authority on racist bullying?

- No. A school's population does not exist in a vacuum away from the rest of society, nor is it unchanging. It would be unrealistic for any school to expect that no racist, sexist or homophobic bullying will ever take place. A nil return from a school might imply that pupils are not confident about reporting incidents to staff, or that staff have not understood the nature or seriousness of prejudice-related incidents.

Will it look bad if a school has a lot of incidents on its return?

- If the reporting procedures work efficiently, an initial increase in the number of incidents reported can be expected, as schools become more successful in communicating their commitment to taking bullying seriously. Subsequently it can be expected that the number of reported incidents will decrease, as schools develop more effective measures for preventing them.

What happens to data that schools provide?

- A local authority is expected to provide an annual report on racist incidents for its own elected members and for schools' governing bodies. They will then be able to compare the pattern at their own school with patterns elsewhere.

Do we have to record small, insignificant incidents?

- Ideally, yes. Every incident, no matter how seemingly small, should be recorded, investigated and dealt with. If offenders and onlookers are permitted to believe prejudice-based bullying is acceptable they may continue with it and become involved later in serious criminal or unlawful activity.

Is racist bullying something that only white people can be guilty of? If so, how do I explain this to the white children at my school and their parents?

- The hallmark of racist bullying in schools is that pupils are attacked as representatives of a group or community, not as individuals. It follows that phrases such as 'white trash' or 'white bitch' are racist and that such taunts or similar sentiments should be dealt with in the same ways as terms such as 'Paki'.

- In all bullying there is a power differential. In the UK as a whole, many though not all minority communities suffer from discrimination and prejudice, and police statistics show that they are much more likely than white people to be targeted by racist attacks. But in the micro-context of a particular school playground or neighbourhood, white people are sometimes in a minority and can be disadvantaged and intimidated by the local balance of power. In these circumstances attacks on them by members of the local majority group should usually be treated as racist bullying.

The most frequent racist incidents at our school involve name-calling. Are certain words always and everywhere inherently racist? Is the word Paki, for example, inherently offensive and objectionable, even when no offence is intended or taken?

■   This is a complex question, since the uses and meanings of language change over time. For example, there are changes in the names which communities find acceptable or not acceptable to describe themselves. Historically, terms such as Paki, Wog, Pikey, Nigger and Kike are racially offensive and cause hurt to the communities to whom they are addressed, since they are almost always used with intent to offend or to vilify.

■   However, in the course of resistance to discrimination communities sometimes reclaim terms which have been used against them, wearing them as badges of pride. For example, the word black has been successfully reclaimed as a positive term. A current example is the use of the word Nigger in African-American rap music. In youth communities sometimes such words are used ironically between people of the same culture, and would not constitute a racist incident. But they should not be used by people outside that culture.

■   Even in the circumstances of reclaiming a word, extreme offence and hurt can be caused. The word Nigger, for example, is a term from slavery and colonialism and continues to be used by far-right organisations in their discourse. Most people from African heritage communities, and especially those from older generations, find it offensive in any and every context. In these circumstances, if young people in school are openly using terms such as Paki or Nigger between themselves the implications should be explained to them.

We have disputes and even fights sometimes between, for example, African-Caribbean pupils and African, or between Sikhs and Muslims, or between pupils who have different national origins, or different locations in a caste system, or different affiliations within the same religion. Should such incidents be treated as racist bullying?

■   If individuals or groups are of equal strength, outbreaks of bad behaviour between them are not normally thought of as bullying. The behaviour is dealt with according to a school's general behaviour policy, not with regard to anti-bullying in particular. If the behaviour includes racist words or stereotypes, or abusive references to others' ethnicity, religion, culture or national origin, the incident should normally be logged as racist, in accordance with the Stephen Lawrence Inquiry definition. Such an incident does not usually, however, carry the undertones of 'you don't belong in this country' which is the hallmark of racist language when used by white people.

■ If there is a power imbalance then almost certainly the incident is an example of bullying, and should be dealt with as such.

■ It is sometimes the case with the kind of incident under discussion here that conflicts in the school are connected to tensions, disagreements and feuds in the neighbourhood. The school has to take action within its own sphere of influence but will almost certainly need to work in partnership with other agencies if there is to be an effective impact in the wider context.

Is physical bullying worse than verbal or psychological bullying?

■ Not necessarily. It is often mistakenly supposed that psychological bullying, name-calling, ignoring and excluding are not as serious as physical violence. However, deep hurt can be inflicted by verbal or psychological bullying that remains with pupils at the receiving end for their whole lives. In recent research, psychologists have reported that memories of painful emotional experiences linger far longer than those involving physical pain. It has also been found that the recollection of such memories inhibits people's ability to perform mental tests more than does the recollection of physical pain. (Association of Psychological Science, 2008).

Prejudice-related incidents

A view is developing in several authorities that not just racist behaviour but behaviour related to all prejudice-related incidents should be monitored. This view is gathering strength as new legal requirements come into force nationally relating to disability, faith or religion, gender and sexual orientation, as a consequence of the Disability Discrimination Act 2005, and the Sex Discrimination Act 1975 as amended by the Equality Act 2006. There will almost certainly be added momentum behind this development through the work of the Equality and Human Rights Commission (EHRC). It appears to be supported by at least one union (NASUWT, 2006).

The possible disadvantage of including a range of prejudice-related behaviour in reporting procedures, not racist behaviour alone, is that the emphasis on racism that followed the Stephen Lawrence Inquiry could be lost or marginalised. Also, there is the danger that the whole exercise could become too cumbersome to be of practical use. The possible advantages, however, include the following. It helps people understand the concept of prejudice-based incidents and bullying so should increase the likelihood of racist behaviour being reported. It makes sense in the day-to-day life of schools – sense to teachers and other staff, and sense also to pupils, parents and governors, for it is easier to explain to children why racist bullying is hurtful and therefore wrong if staff also explain why bullying around gender, disability and sexuality is hurtful and wrong. It removes one of the reasons for current resistance to recording and reporting racist incidents, namely the voice that says: 'Why only concentrate on racism? Why not be concerned about children whose lives are made a misery because of teasing about a disability? Or who get harassed sexually, or are targets of homophobic bullying and insults?'

Racism is not the same as sexism or homophobia or hostility towards disabled people. But the measures required to prevent racism are similar to the measures required to prevent other forms of prejudice-related behaviour. So are the measures to deal with incidents when they occur. A holistic approach to all prejudice-related incidents is clearly consonant with what earlier in this book was described in chapter 4 and commended as the restorative or transformative approach to dealing with incidents.

The current legal requirement is to record all racist incidents, regardless of their seriousness, and simply on the basis of whether they are 'perceived' to be racist. Aggregating all incidents together or distinguishing only between physical and verbal behaviour is likely to produce unreliable and unhelpful statistics. An approach being piloted in at least one authority is to use a four-point scale, as follows:

- No offence was intended or taken
- Hurt or distress was caused, but the offending behaviour is unlikely to be repeated
- Hurt or distress was caused, and the pupils responsible had previously been warned that their behaviour was unacceptable
- Substantial hurt or distress was caused; the behaviour was based on substantial hostility and prejudice; the behaviour may be repeated.

Most authorities require schools to report the nature of incidents against a list ranging from name-calling to physical violence. It is also worth collecting and publishing data about time of day, the date and to ask about corridors, playgrounds and journeys to and from school. In addition, reports at local authority level need to provide a breakdown by geographical areas, preferably aligned with districts used by the police, so that possible convergences and discrepancies between educational and police data can be identified.

Several authorities have found it is helpful to complement written reporting (whether paper-based or electronic) with professional conversations and/or interview-based surveys. Such conversations and interviews are likely to produce more useful (though softer) data with regard to decision-making and policy-making. At school level, staff may similarly get a better feel for what is going on amongst pupils by asking them directly in conversation or focus groups, rather than waiting for complaints to be made. This point is vividly illustrated in chapter 2 of this book. Some authorities, as has been mentioned, routinely include questions about bullying, including racist bullying, in their annual surveys of pupil voice. So do some schools. Both these approaches may yield more useful data than recording forms do on their own.

Concluding note

Legal requirements and expectations relating to the recording and reporting of racist incidents in schools can be experienced as no more than bureaucratic and mechanistic chores; can fail to produce data of practical use; and can bring the essential task of preventing and addressing racism in education into disrepute. Yet they have substantial potential and this is particularly likely to be achieved when systems are part and parcel of a restorative and transformative approach to dealing with incidents (see chapter 4), and when they are integrated with the overall school curriculum. What key ideas and concepts should be taught across the curriculum in all subjects, and to all learners of all ages? What questions should be asked in reviews and evaluations? What are the practical opportunities for direct and indirect teaching in each subject? These and similar questions are the subject of the next chapter.

6

The needs of a diverse society
Changing and developing the curriculum

The Stephen Lawrence Inquiry (Macpherson, 1999) made 70 recommendations, most of them (66) to do with dealing with incidents by the criminal justice system. The other four were concerned with the prevention of racism, as distinct from dealing with incidents when they occur and three of these were to do with the role of the education system. They referred to the curriculum, the responsibilities of schools and local authorities, and the role of Ofsted. The one concerning the curriculum was that:

> ■ consideration be given to amendment of the national curriculum aimed at valuing cultural diversity and preventing racism, in order better to reflect the needs of a diverse society. (Macpherson, 1999: 334)

This chapter is about how the education system has responded. The recurring problem has been that valuing cultural diversity and preventing racism are not the same. Both are essential but it is all too possible to undertake the one without the other. It is possible, for example, to learn about another culture without learning about the lived experience of racism that people of that culture suffer in their daily lives. Further, as was well said almost 20 years before the Stephen Lawrence report was published, 'just to learn about other people's cultures is not to learn about the racism of one's own. To learn about the racism of one's own culture, on the other hand, is to approach other cultures objectively' (Sivanandan, 1980). Also, to learn about racisms and their dynamics and consequences, and how to challenge, reduce and remove them, does not logically require, in theory or necessarily in practice, learning about other cultures.

The problem began on day one, with the government's official response to the Stephen Lawrence Inquiry. Issued on 23 March 1999, within five weeks of the publication of the Inquiry, it was entirely about valuing cultural diversity in schools and made not the slightest reference to preventing racism. The discourse was all of 'the diverse nature of British society' ... 'the contributions of different countries and cultures' ... fostering 'an understanding of the diversity of cultures which exists in Britain today' and the curriculum's role in 'developing pupils' knowledge and understanding of different beliefs and cultures, including an appreciation of diversity' (Home Office, 1999:33). Near total silence about racism was a feature of the work of the Qualifications and Curriculum Authority (QCA) during the following years, and in a sequence of documents published by the DfES on citizenship education and community cohesion (see Osler and Starkey, 2005; Osler, 2008).

The government's silence was finally broken by a section in a document about race equality in mainly white schools (DfES, 2004), reprinted in guidance on countering bullying around racism, culture and religion two years later (DfES, 2006) and incorporated into the government-funded CREAM project (Coles, 2008). These documents and projects were non-statutory and were not widely disseminated or publicised. They did, however, have a certain moral force. They were complemented and amplified by guidance developed by local authorities, for example Cambridgeshire (Rees, 2003), Derbyshire (Richardson, 2004), Newham (Bednall *et al*, 2007), Hampshire (Theodore, 2004) and City of Nottingham (Daffé, 2005), and by voluntary sector organisations such as Kick It Out (2007, and see chapter 8) and the Runnymede Trust (Runnymede, 2003). Some of these projects and publications are described below.

First it is relevant to consider an objection that is sometimes made: 'we must first and foremost teach basic skills – we simply do not have time to include issues of culture and racism as well'. The story is told that a principal inspector in a large shire authority which includes not only largely white rural areas but also inner city multiethnic areas, was alarmed when he was interviewing a candidate to design and organise a substantial programme of inservice training for the local authority's teachers. 'If we were to appoint you,' he said, 'isn't there a danger that you would bring multicultural into everything?' This chapter is a riposte to that inspector. The key points are:

■ Education is not a narrow concept concerned with imparting facts. To educate the whole child teachers must be concerned with ethics, values and principles, amongst which are equality, justice, caring and respect for self and others.

■ Recognising and respecting pupils' identities, stories and back-grounds helps them to feel secure and self-confident. It necessarily involves not colluding with the notions of white superiority which fuelled racism in the past and affirm those who bully on racist grounds in the present. Children who feel safe, comfortable and in-cluded in their environment are in the optimum state to learn. Tackl-ing racist bullying has everything to do with education and learning. There is no contradiction between 'bringing multicultural into every-thing' and promoting high standards.

■ This principle applies not only to pupils who are at the receiving end of bullying but also to those who are responsible. Unhappiness, low self-esteem and poor educational achievement may underlie their behaviour.

■ There are no circumstances under which it would be appropriate to take a monocultural one-size-fits-all approach, or to teach about Britain as if it were not part of a global society.

Key concepts and questions across the curriculum

As mentioned, the DfES website on countering racist bullying (DfES, 2006a) republished material from a document on mainly-white schools (DfES, 2004). The concern was to identify ideas relevant to preventing racism that should be taught and learned at all age levels, and directly or indirectly in all subjects. A broadly similar approach had been pioneered internationally by James Banks and colleagues (Banks *et al*, 2005). The DfES proposed six such ideas, to do with shared humanity, difference and diversity, identity and belonging, global interdependence, excellence everywhere, and racial justice. Only the sixth and last of these themes is directly and explicitly about racism. It is nevertheless related to, and dependent on, the other five.

First, the DfES guidance stressed shared humanity: the feelings, strivings, aspirations and anxieties that all human beings have in common by virtue of being human. Second, and in tandem, it stressed difference and diversity, and contrasting stories and interpretations. Third, the guidance then referred to issues of personal identity and belonging and to notions of Britishness. It said:

> Every individual belongs to a range of different groups, and therefore has a range of different loyalties and affiliations. Also, and partly in consequence, all individuals change and develop. Pupils need to know and feel confident in their own identity but also to be open to change and development, and to be able to engage positively

with other identities. All pupils need to be comfortable with the concept of multiple identities and with hyphenated terms such as Black-British, British-Muslim and English-British. (DfES, 2004:21)

Some years later these points were endorsed by the DfES Diversity and Citizenship Curriculum Review (Ajegbo, 2006). The fourth key concept was global interdependence, and borrowing, mingling and mutual influence. A recurring danger in teaching and learning about cultures is that pupils will get the idea that each culture is distinct from all others. The reality is that boundaries between cultures are porous and frequently unclear. In any case there are issues in the modern world which can only be understood if they are seen as part of a single world system, and which have to be addressed through international cooperation. A sense of global interdependence is a vital component of cosmopolitan citizenship (Osler and Starkey, 2005; Appiah, 2006). Fifth, the guidance pointed out that excellence is to be found in all cultures, societies and traditions, not in 'the west' only. The default position in the curriculum, however, can all too often be the assumption that all significant human achievements arose in the West.

The sixth cluster of key concepts was to do with race, ethnicity and racism. Already at key stage 1, the guidance said, pupils need to appreciate there is a single race, the human race, but that the world contains ignorance, prejudice, discrimination and injustice. In the course of their time at school pupils should become familiar with theories about the sources and forms of racism, including individual racism and institutional racism. They need also, the DfES guidance continued, to know about strategies, actions and campaigns to prevent and address racism, locally, nationally and internationally; equal opportunities in employment and the provision of services; the role of legislation; conflict resolution and restorative justice; intercultural communication and relationships; and justice and fairness. Not least, they need to know what they themselves can do to tackle racism within their own sphere of influence, for example racist bullying and behaviour in and around their own school. A close study of educational projects aimed at challenging and changing racist attitudes amongst young people (Lemos, 2005) has shown that effectiveness depends on there being a range of activities, presenters and facilitators; sustained activities over a period of time; reflection on personal attitudes and experiences; enquiry into local events and circumstances; learning through doing and experiencing, not just listening and talking; and establishing common ground and shared values and interests.

The CREAM Project (Curriculum Reflecting the Experience of African-Caribbean and Muslim pupils) built on the DfES key concepts outlined above but presented them as questions and added a few points. These included:

- Does the curriculum counteract over-simplified, stereotypical views by teaching that, within every cultural tradition, there is a diversity of viewpoints, lifestyle and beliefs?

- Does the curriculum teach that every culture interprets its history through certain grand narratives and that these, in turn, contribute to the identities of individuals?

- Does the curriculum give status to the experiences and achievement of people from backgrounds and cultures that pupils value?

- Does the curriculum teach that societies and the cultures within them are constantly changing and developing? Does it teach that there is not a fixed, static view or perspective for a cultural group in any time or place?

The CREAM project asked its questions about the coverage of Islam in the curriculum in relation to every national curriculum subject and at each key stage (Coles, 2008: chapter 2).

Teaching about bias and standpoints

Anyone teaching in the 1980s may still have tucked away somewhere at the back of a drawer, a badge bearing the legend 'Teach the Children the Truth'. Teaching the children the truth is an aim no one would disagree with. The problem is that truth is frequently a reflection of a standpoint. It depends not only on facts but on experiences, cultures, beliefs, stories handed down, politics, personalities and material interests. The story of a violent conflict, most obviously, is told differently according to which side the narrator is on. Conflicting narratives relating to Israel/Palestine, for example, have been presented at length by the Glasgow University Media Group (Philo and Barry, 2004) and by Bhikhu Parekh in relation to Islam and 'the West' (Parekh, 2008). Conflicting views of a stage in the development of modern South Africa are shown overleaf in table 6.1, by way of an example.

For many years the second narrative was taught in schools in South Africa and was explicit in all the textbooks. It not only reflected but also legitimised and reinforced the world view that underlay the structural racism of the apartheid system. With the overturn of apartheid came a new curriculum and new textbooks which challenge and deconstruct the earlier narrative and replace

---

Box 6.1: Conflicting narratives about a stage in South African history

Narrative A	Narrative B
The San people were peaceful hunter gathers and herders. They held no concept of land ownership: the land belonged to everyone. Everyone settled where they found fertile land and water and farmed according to their needs.	The Boers from Holland came to settle in South Africa. They were brave pioneers, the Voortrekkers. They endured hardships to set up their own settlements.
They welcomed strangers into their community and expected them to live with the same values.	The people they found in the land were uncivilised natives, the bushmen.
They were shocked when the strangers they had welcomed began to fence off parts of the San people's land and fought off the San to prevent access to it.	When they established their farms and settlements and put boundaries on their land, they consistently had to fight off the savage bushmen from going onto it.

---

it with a view that is historically more accurate and substantially more consistent with the values underpinning the South African Constitution adopted on 4 December 1996, following the interim constitution of 1993. There is further discussion of competing and overlapping narratives in chapter 10 ('Pictures of the world in the mind's eye').

Direct and indirect teaching

The taught curriculum should certainly include direct teaching about key ideas such as those outlined above. Direct approaches are particularly likely in citizenship, English, history, PSHE and RE, but these will be less effective if not placed in the context of the inclusive school where the ethos and curriculum are based on the principles of promoting equality and justice. The policy and practice of developing such an ethos can be described as indirect teaching. The relationship between a) creating a positive, inclusive school ethos b) combating racism and c) raising achievement is one of interdependence: Each has a positive effect on each of the others.

The tables on the following pages give examples of how national curriculum targets can be taught using both indirect and direct approaches in mathematics, physical education and dance, and science. These three subjects have been chosen because it is sometimes supposed that they do not contain opportunities for valuing diversity and preventing racism.

The English National Curriculum at Key Stages 2 and 3:
Targets which are relevant and contribute to combating racism

National curriculum

Mathematics key stage 3	Indirect approach	Direct approach
Processing, representing and interpreting data **2) Pupils should be taught to:** ■ solve problems involving data ■ interpret tables, lists and charts used in everyday life; construct and interpret frequency tables, including tables for grouped discrete data ■ represent and interpret discrete data using graphs and diagrams, including pictograms, bar charts and line graphs, then interpret a wider range of graphs and diagrams, using ICT where appropriate ■ know that mode is a measure of average and that range is a measure of spread, and to use both ideas to describe data sets	2) Knowing how to process, represent and interpret data makes an important contribution to antiracist teaching. Pupils should be taught how to use data to get the information they need. They can also learn how to select the data they need to win a debate. Pupils can also be shown that data can be presented in ways that are mischievously misleading.	Teachers can choose a research, data-handling and interpretation project to get information to support antiracism. Examples include information on local and national young communities using statistical data, surveys of pupil opinion and experience of identified issues of interest and concern, making graphical representations of actual information on refugee and asylum-seeking communities as a 'myth-busting' exercise, discussing and analysing research reports on national issues, reports on government information etc.

National curriculum	Indirect approach	Direct approach
■ recognise the difference between discrete and continuous data ■ draw conclusions from statistics and graphs and recognise when information is presented in a misleading way; explore doubt and certainty and develop an understanding of probability through classroom situations; discuss events using a vocabulary that includes the words 'equally likely', 'fair', 'unfair', 'certain'. **Breadth of study** **1) During the key stage, pupils should be taught the Knowledge, skills and understanding through:** ■ activities that extend their understanding of the number system to include integers, fractions and decimals ■ using patterns and relationships to explore simple algebraic ideas ■ drawing inferences from data in practical activities, and recognising the difference between meaningful and misleading representations of data	In teaching about number systems, algebra and geometry the teacher should include the contribution made by mathematicians from Africa and Asia from early history to the present day.	

National curriculum	Indirect approach	Direct approach
Physical Education **Key stage 2**		
Breadth of study **5) During the key stage, pupils should** **be taught the Knowledge, skills and** **understanding through five areas of** **activity:** a. dance activities b. games activities c. gymnastic activities *and two activity areas from:* d. swimming activities and water safety e. athletic activities f. outdoor and adventurous activities. Swimming activities and water safety must be chosen as one of these areas of activity unless pupils have completed the full key stage 2 teaching requirements in relation to swimming activities and water safety during key stage 1.	All pupils are entitled to participate in the PE national curriculum, and are expected to do so. It is very important for schools to enable pupils who belong to all religious backgrounds to participate. Schools today provide uniform options for PE that are acceptable to all communities and conform to health and safety regulations. There should be separate changing facilities for girls and boys, and somewhere private to change if this is required. It is rare for schools and parents not to be able to come to an acceptable arrangement to ensure that pupils can participate fully. Schools should be sensitive at times such as Ramadan, where some pupils even in the primary school may be fasting. It is not safe to insist that they take part in strenuous activities if they are not able to, and they should certainly not be made to	Teachers and pupils could agree an explicit code of practice in which racist comments are not allowed, and incur penalties. There is concern about the lack of Asian players coming forward in the football league, both men and women. There is also concern about the lack of black football managers.

National curriculum	Indirect approach	Direct approach
	take part in activities which might place them in danger, such as using PE equipment. At these times it is very important for pupils to feel that the school is supportive of them, and not to feel excluded. They should be given meaningful activities (rather than being left to sit in a corridor) and praised for the effort they are making for Ramadan. The activities could be related to the PE curriculum, such as researching and writing about famous athletes, preparing a useful list of the rules of football or any other game, clear enough to be shared with their peers etc. The nature and importance of Ramadan should be explained to the class and to school staff, including administrative and support staff. Teachers should note that the DCSF fully understands the issue of primary school children fasting for Ramadan.	Teachers could take steps to redress these concerns for the young people they are working with. They could take targeted action to include Asian pupils in football, and to develop them and black pupils in team leading capacities.

National curriculum	Indirect approach	Direct approach
Dance activities	5) and 6)	Schools should make sure that staff are aware of the inaccuracy of the many myths surrounding people from different backgrounds in sport: myths such as African and African Caribbean communities not being able to swim because they sink in the water, or that South Asian boys cannot play football because they are not strong enough, scared of the weather, do not have the right diet etc.
6) Pupils should be taught to:	Dance and music activities from a range of cultures are required in the national curriculum.	
a. create and perform dances using a range of movement: patterns, including those from differen: times, places and cultures		
b. respond to a range of stimuli and accompaniment.		
Swimming activities and water safety	Pupils should be able to wear clothing to enable them to participate in swimming if their family's religious belief requires them for example to keep their legs covered. This includes allowing them to change in private.	
Outdoor and adventurous activities	Pupils could also have the opportunity to try games from a range of cultures.

Kabbadi, played widely in South and East Asia, is a popular example, and it needs no equipment. | |

National curriculum	Direct approach	Indirect approach
Science key stage 3 **Ideas and evidence in science** 1) Pupils should be taught: ■ about the interplay between empirical questions, evidence and scientific explanations using historical and contemporary examples [for example, Lavoisier's work on burning, the possible causes of global warming] ■ that it is important to test explanations by using them to make predictions and by seeing if evidence matches the predictions ■ about the ways in which scientists work today and how they worked in the past, including the roles of experimentation, evidence and creative thought in the development of scientific ideas. **Humans as organisms** 2) Pupils should be taught: about the need for a balanced diet containing carbohydrates, proteins, fats, minerals, vitamins, fibre and water, and about foods that are sources of these	1) It is important to give examples of contributions of scientists from across the world, and not just from Britain or Europe. Teachers will be able to find information on black scientists and inventors by researching the web. Information on books available can be obtained from specialist bookshops supplying books to reflect black, Asian and other ethnic communities. 2) Foods being investigated should include food from a range of countries and communities, for example yam or sweet potato for carbohydrates, kiwi fruit and guava for vitamins etc.	Pupils could research and write about great scientists from history and across the world. The writing could be made into books which can be kept as classroom resources. Specific work could be done on black scientists and inventors for Black History Month (October,) on scientist and inventors from refugee communities for refugee week (June) on Muslim scientists and inventors at Ramadan and so on. The dates of special focuses should be regarded as a starting point only, and the work should become integrated into the mainstream curriculum of the school. There are websites where pupils can access information on scientists and inventors.

It is also crucially relevant to note that key ideas such as those mentioned above are learned experientially through the ways a school and its classrooms are structured and organised. In this connection the Rights Respecting Schools (RRS) project, pioneered internationally by Unease, is worth particular mention. Research has shown that in the UK as in other countries (Howe and Covill, 2007) the project leads to:

- improved pupil self-esteem

- enhanced moral development

- improved behaviour and relationships

- more positive attitudes towards diversity in society

- increased global awareness

- reduction of prejudice

- active citizenship, locally, nationally and globally

- less bullying and truancy

- more readiness by pupils to be assertive in intervening and mediating in bullying situations.

Concluding note: the role of Ofsted

This chapter is about just one of the Lawrence Inquiry's recommendations on education. It also recommended that school governing bodies and local authorities should be given a legal duty to prevent and address racism. This was duly implemented through the race equality duty (RED) in the Race Relations (Amendment) Act 2000. A third was that Ofsted inspections should examine implementation of the first two. Potentially, this was of great significance and value. In practice, however, it has proved unsatisfactory.

Research undertaken shortly after the Lawrence Inquiry report found that inspectors were 'ill-equipped to carry out the task' (Osler and Starkey, 2005:172, summarising Osler and Morrison, 2002). In autumn 2007, shortly before it became part of the Equality and Human Rights Commission (EHRC), the Commission for Racial Equality (CRE) reported that Ofsted 'has the poorest record of any inspection or regulatory body. It does not accept that it has a responsibility to monitor RED [race equality duty] performance of public authorities within its arena of responsibility. It is arguably the most unco-operative public authority the Commission has had to deal with over the last two years' (Johnson and McCarvill, 2007:39). It is difficult to imagine a more damning judgement. The CRE also judged that Ofsted's latest race equality scheme, dated summer 2007, was still non-compliant with legislation.

In summer 2008, however, Ofsted republished its race equality scheme in a revised version and explicitly acknowledged for the first time that the race equality duty covers how it uses its influence: 'Equality and diversity are at the heart of what we do and how we do it: our commitment is reflected in our practice internally and in *all aspects of our influence and work in inspection and regulation*' (Ofsted, 2008: paragraph 1.3.2, emphasis added). This presumably meets with the approval of the Equality and Human Rights Commission, though the scheme makes no explicit acknowledgement that Ofsted needs to assess how schools address and prevent racism, or even how they value cultural diversity. In summer 2008, examination of a small but representative sample of recently published reports showed that 23 out of 28 contained no comment or evidence about racism, racist incidents, racist bullying or a race equality policy and that 25 out of 28 made no comment on the role of the curriculum in preventing and addressing racism. Inspectors commented in general terms on harmonious and cohesive communities, and on pupils being safe and happy. These are worthy and important achievements, but they do not cast light on whether the school (or the inspector) pays any heed to racist incidents and racist bullying. The potential influence of Ofsted remains as yet unfulfilled. Meanwhile, there are many valuable projects in which schools can be involved, as described in the chapters that follow.

7

Emotive and controversial history
Principles to adopt, pitfalls to avoid

The year 2007 saw the 200th anniversary of the British parliament passing the Act to abolish the transatlantic slave trade. In the same year a government report on the teaching of history commented that 'the way teachers handle emotive and controversial history can have a negative impact on pupils' (Historical Association 2007:15). It explained that recent research on the impact of teaching about the transatlantic slave trade and its abolition at key stage 3 had shown that portraying black people as victims can make African-Caribbean pupils and their parents feel alienated and disconnected. It also pointed out that white working-class pupils in certain educational settings can feel alienated if the role of white abolitionists in the process of abolition is so downplayed that all credit for ending the slave trade is given to economic factors and to black resistance. This chapter discusses practical ways to overcome such difficulties.

Amid the flurry of activity to commemorate the Act and those who took part in the fight to achieve it, and to demand or proffer apologies for the hideous trade, demand swelled for it to be included in the national curriculum in England and Wales. This demand was partly born from a recognition that modern society and the experience of black communities can only be understood in a full historical context which includes the transatlantic slave trade, and that the transatlantic slave trade is one of the foundation stones of racism. 'Slavery was not born of racism,' runs a well-known dictum. 'Rather, racism was the consequence of slavery' (Williams, 1964, quoted in Commission on the Future of Multi-Ethnic Britain, 2000:73).

In February 2007 the government issued a statement about a revised national curriculum for England and Wales. The key stage 3 history curriculum would include the study of the transatlantic slave trade and abolitionists such as William Wilberforce and Oluadah Equiano. It would help pupils understand such concepts as the story of the British Empire and their own identities. Details of the new secondary curriculum were announced in a statement on 2 July 2007. It would be phased in between September 2008 and September 2010, starting with key stage 3, in which the transatlantic slave trade would be taught. It was also announced that pupils would learn about shared British values and study national identity in the UK through the prism of history and this would include coverage of the legacy of the British Empire.

The proposal met with strong reactions from the right and the left of the political spectrum. Many educationalists and antiracists welcomed it and thought it long overdue; others complained that the history curriculum was being taken over by woolly political ideas and social engineering. Some African and Caribbean organisations which had long demanded that the curriculum reflect a full and true picture of African history greeted the news with caution.

Why are many black communities expressing concern about including the transatlantic slave trade in the national curriculum? And what has it got to do with racist bullying? The answer is that teaching and learning are not just about the content of the curriculum but also about the understandings and views of the teacher. If they are taught by someone who has not given thought to potential implicit messages even the best-intentioned initiatives can be seriously damaging. The likelihood of damaging impact is not without precedent. Young black people recall squirming uncomfortably in classes where their peers learned that 'people in Ghana wore grass skirts and lived in mud huts until the white man came with intermediate technology'. They were required to write essays with this information, and were taunted in the playground.

White pupils had their worst stereotypes confirmed. One of the pupils quoted in chapter 2 wrote: 'The overriding feeling was a sense of injustice at the fact that everything about the content and structure of the curriculum seemed to be saying that black people are worthless at best, never had amounted to anything and never would without the white man.' More recently it has been reported that following lessons teaching about the transatlantic slave trade, a pupil was physically and verbally assaulted and had the word 'slave 04' written on his back. When he retaliated to continuing bullying, he was reported to the police and charged with actual bodily harm. Already in 2008 there was anecdotal evidence of pupils being subject to taunts of 'slave' in the playground, bullied as a result of insensitive and poorly informed teaching.

This is not entirely surprising, given that teachers are being expected to teach something they themselves did not learn in school, and which was not included in their teacher training programme. To date teacher training establishments have largely ignored the subject. In 2008 the teachers and teacher trainers who have learned about the transatlantic slave are most likely to have learned it from textbooks written from a colonial perspective. The jingoistic story of the British Empire generally promoted in textbooks in the past is a far cry from the story of the British Empire envisaged in the new citizenship curriculum, and there is much work to do to catch up with current insights.

The DfES Diversity and Citizenship Curriculum Review (Ajegbo, 2006) raised similar concerns. It commented that:

- discrimination based on racial hierarchies has not disappeared and stereotypes still exist in society

- many teachers do not see the link between their subject and education for diversity, do not know how to deal with it and are hampered by insufficient resources or training in how to use them effectively

- schools do not recognise the clear link between the promotion of education for diversity and the raising of educational standards.

Teaching the transatlantic slave trade well can make a strong contribution to the development of students' commitment to justice and understanding and to combating racism. Taught appropriately, the topic contributes to the school's duty under the Race Relations Act to promote race equality. It affirms the achievement of African communities and people of African descent and helps to reduce racist bullying.

Although the new national curriculum regulations place the transatlantic slave trade in the history curriculum at key stage 3 the topic can be an integral part of other curriculum areas as well. Aspects of it will fit within PSHE and citizenship and the contextual topic of African civilisations has content relevant to English, art and design, science and mathematics. There is considerable scope for drama and for pupils to write in different modes.

As with all sensitive issues, however, it is vital for teachers to be well prepared before embarking on the topic, and to have a framework for teaching it. The ten principles set out in box 7.1 are intended to help teachers develop a relevant framework and content. They advocate approaches which fit within and enhance the context of combating racism in education and of developing inclusive schools. The principles have been honed to focus sharply on the transatlantic slave trade; related topics, such as present day slavery, have intentionally not been included in order to keep the focus.

Box 7.1: Ten principles for teaching about the transatlantic slave trade

1   Make sure that every child in your class can maintain their dignity and self-esteem during the teaching of this topic.

2   Do not approach the topic from a deficit model position of 'poor, helpless black people in Africa and the Caribbean'.

3   Make sure that the resources you use do not compound a deficit model.

4   Make sure the pupils understand about great African civilisations. Never start with African people as slaves.

5   Teach the pupils the complex nature of cruelty in the transatlantic slave trade and plantation life.

6   Include the stories of African heritage leaders of rebellion and opposition in the Caribbean.

7   Include the stories of freed enslaved Africans and servants in Europe who took part in the fight for abolition.

8   Include the stories of white abolitionists as role models in the fight against injustice and racism, but do not imply that only white people were responsible for the abolition.

9   Place the topic in a context of human rights.

10 Take care of your own professional development beforehand. This is a sensitive issue.

---

1 Make sure that every child in your class can maintain their dignity and self-esteem during the teaching of this topic

All the principles contribute to this crucial aim.

African heritage pupils, particularly those from the Caribbean, are most at risk of being made to feel uncomfortable and lose dignity and self-esteem. Never teach so that the first impression, or worse still the only impression, of people of African heritage is of helpless, abject enslavement. However, neither is it helpful to imply that all white people supported the evils of slavery and its legacy, nor that all white people today are responsible for the crimes, negligence, ignorance and injustice of their forebears. All pupils should be involved in all activities, and African heritage pupils should not be singled out.

Be aware of the potential for some pupils to make inappropriate comments, and if that happens, deal with the situation quickly.

Get a display up as quickly as possible showing positive images associated with the project. You could do this with commercially produced materials and posters before the project starts rather than wait for them to be introduced in the work. The pupils' own work can be displayed later. Contemporaneous engravings of abject Africans in chains and degrading situations abound in materials for teaching about the transatlantic slave trade. It is appropriate for pupils to see them, but take care not to have them as the initial images or the pervading images around the classroom. Where they are used in the classroom, it must be in the context of discussion of the context in which they were produced.

2 Do not approach the subject from a deficit model position of 'poor helpless black people in Africa and the Caribbean'

The pupils should be confident in a positive concept of people of African heritage, whether it is taught as part of the topic or whether it has been taught previously (for example in Black History Month) or as part of the history or citizenship curricula. Ideally, and for best practice, this concept should be enshrined automatically in an inclusive curriculum.

This is not as obvious as it seems, because not all teaching resources take an inclusive approach. For example, resources for teaching about the Victorians often ignore the presence of black people in England, and resources for teaching about great figures in science, literature and the arts often ignore the contributions of black people. It is important to find appropriate resources in all curriculum areas.

3 Make sure that the resources you use do not compound a deficit model

School resources should celebrate and affirm identity and diversity and provide a balanced and inclusive representation of world history and culture. In evaluating resources for teaching about the transatlantic slave trade, the following questions could be considered:

- Do the illustrations and content reflect perspectives of a range of different communities, as opposed to a Eurocentric viewpoint?

- Do the illustrations and content allow pupils and communities dignity and respect?

- Do they extend pupils' knowledge of the world society and inter-dependence?

- Do they include first hand accounts from enslaved Africans writing about their experience, and arguments from abolitionists?

To source the study, make use of the websites set up by black organisations specifically for this topic and make a point of using one of the many specialist suppliers of books, and support any local black bookshops. Such booksellers are committed to providing positive images. They know what is available and will willingly help schools put together appropriate collections.

4 Make sure the pupils understand about great African civilisations. Never start with African people as slaves

There are many civilisations all over Africa which you could choose to teach about. For example, materials developed for schools in one London borough focused on the Akan and Benin empires – not only because of their achievements and cultures, but because most of the enslaved Africans taken to the Caribbean (and therefore ancestors of pupils in English schools) came from that region of West Africa.

5 Teach the pupils the complex nature of cruelty in the transatlantic slave trade and plantation life

Concepts to be taught are:

- the horrendous physical cruelty of branding, gagging, chains, whipping and more

- the emotional cruelty, stealing people from Africa, separating families including mothers and children, treating people as chattels to be bought and sold

■ that the horrific treatment of enslaved Africans was refined and institutionalised for profit. The concept of calculated cruelties such as the way the enslaved Africans were packed into the slave ships, and decisions made on balancing the profits slavers could make if they 'packed' ships with so many slaves that they would expect a certain number of them to die, or if they had slightly fewer numbers but less deaths at sea

■ the financial reasons which contributed to the abolition of the trans-atlantic slave trade

■ the family fortunes and cities which were founded on the proceeds of the transatlantic slave trade.

6 Include the stories of African heritage leaders of rebellion and opposition in the Caribbean

'They will remember that we were sold but they won't remember that we were strong. They will remember that we were bought, but not that we were brave.' Thus wrote William Prescott, former enslaved African, in 1937, quoted by Linda Ali in her article for the *Set All Free* website.

It is crucial to make sure that the role of enslaved Africans in securing their own freedom is properly emphasised. Thousands of enslaved Africans took part in uprisings and contributed to the struggle for freedom. In teaching about plantation life, include resistance as well as rebellion. Enslaved Africans developed important forms of resistance by finding ways of keeping alive African cultures, stories, beliefs and forms of worship, and languages. Running away was another form of resistance, and often important rebellions were carried out by communities of runaway enslaved Africans such as Nanny and the Maroons in Jamaica.

If you have pupils in your class with family backgrounds from a particular island in the Caribbean, research the stories of rebellion on their island. There is probably not a single island on which slave resistance did not take place. You will find a comprehensive list of rebellions and their leaders at : http://caribbean-guide.info/past.and.present/history/slave.rebellion/index.html. In addition, the websites of Caribbean governments often include relevant information in their history sections. Jamaica is a good example, providing clear information on Jamaica's national heroes.

7 Include the stories of freed enslaved Africans and servants in Europe who took part in the fight for abolition

It is important to include the presence and contributions of African people in Britain throughout the curriculum, but it is absolutely essential in teaching about the transatlantic slave trade.

There were many people of African descent living in Britain and Europe who took part in the overall fight against slavery and in the abolition movement in Britain. Their own writings and writings about them are readily available. They include such people as Olaudah Equiano, Ignatius Sancho and Ottobah Cugoano. A good starting point for finding information about them, and white abolitionists too, is Brycchan Carey's website at http://www.brycchan carey.com/abolition/index.htm.

8 Include the stories of white abolitionists as role models in the fight against injustice and racism, but do not imply that only white people were responsible for the abolition

In Britain there has been a national focus on the role of William Wilberforce, who led the passing of the Abolition of Slavery Act. However, thousands of British men and women contributed to the campaign against slavery, especially through abolition societies, politics or the churches. Pupils need to know that there were white role models in the fight for freedom and justice. Wherever possible relate the teaching content to the local contexts of area and heritage, so that it is meaningful to the pupils in your class.

Information can be found about black people living throughout Britain in the period being studied. In some areas research has been done, for example by London Metropolitan Archives in the London area, by the libraries service in Oxfordshire, at the National Maritime Museum in Greenwich, and slave trails in Bristol and Liverpool. Documents such as parish registers and church-wardens' accounts can also yield fascinating information. It is interesting, for example, to compare the baptism entries of black people, which usually do not have the precise age and family details that are included in entries for white people. You can get a flavour of the kind of information available from the entries in Box 7.2, researched in one London borough.

In the local context there may be information about the history of notable local families whose fortunes were made through slave plantations. In Liverpool and Bristol for example, this information is readily available, but in other areas the borough archivist may already have the information or be willing to help research it. There may also have been abolitionists living in the local area.

Box 7.2: Local evidence

Examples of evidence of black people living in one local area, researched from churchwardens' accounts records held at the borough archive, and from parish registers researched and published by the London Metropolitan Archive

---

Gave two slaves 6 pence

Entry in churchwardens' accounts for the Parish of Norwood
Accounts of Mr Charles Stokes and Mr William Coker, May 9 1744

Gave 7 slaves 1 shilling

Entry in churchwardens' accounts for the Parish of Norwood
Accounts of Mr Rich, Gilbert, May 16 1745

Borough: *Ealing*　　　**Parish**: *Saint Mary, Ealing*
Father's First Name:
Mother's First Name:
Date Baptised: *29 Dec 1721*
Householder:
Notes:

*Henry – a Black abt the age of 7, baptised Decr 24.
Sponsors:James Welch, Edward Hughes, & Hannah Robins 1721*

Borough: *Ealing*　　　**Parish**: *Saint Mary, Ealing*
Father's First Name:
Mother's First Name:
Date Baptised: *09 Jun 1779*
Householder:
Notes:

Johnson, Laetitia – a negro woman aged about twenty eight years baptised June 9th

9 Place the topic in a context of human rights

Teaching about the transatlantic slave trade from a human rights perspective places it within a context which pupils can understand today and in which the dignity of humankind is respected.

10 Take care of your own professional development beforehand. This is a sensitive issue

Teaching about the transatlantic slave trade requires a sensitive approach. Teaching about racism is sensitive too, and teachers are often not confident with it. With older pupils, teaching about the transatlantic slave trade can also lead to discussion of controversial issues, such as whether there should be reparations. It all requires careful preparation.

Getting the teaching approach right is crucial. Only then can the learning outcome lead to an understanding of racism and the importance of combating it. Only then can it be ensured that the topic confronts and combats racism and does not compound it.

Box 7.4: Parents and community organisations

Sometimes parents are concerned about this topic being taught – and justifiably so, given that in the past it has been taught using the deficit model approach which is so damaging to the image of people of African heritage.

For schools which have easy and ongoing discussions with parents on curriculum issues, it should present no problem to have the discussion about what you are intending to teach and how you are going to approach it. For schools which do not have a current channel of communication with parents on such issues, the topic might offer the opportunity of opening it. However, the topic should not be blown up as something extra or different. It is just part of the school curriculum.

Many areas have community organisations such as supplementary schools, parents' organisations or racial equality councils which will support this work.

Concluding note

'They will remember that we were sold but they won't remember that we were strong. They will remember that we were bought, but not that we were brave.'

This chapter has discussed teaching a sensitive and challenging area of history from an antiracist approach. However, as shown in chapter 6, education to combat racism is not confined to emotive and controversial topics in history: rather it is a thread running throughout the curriculum. In addition to the teaching approaches described in this chapter, there is a need to teach about racism itself. Chapter 8 provides support for teachers through using the motivation of popular culture.

8

A big problem, not just in football but in life
Classroom and school projects

'Kick this evil out of the beautiful game' ... 'I'm lucky because as a white person, I've never experienced the kind of racism some Black people suffer' ... 'All people will come up against barriers in life. The first thing you think is 'I don't deserve this.' But you have to be determined to overcome it' ... 'I've seen the footage on television of when racism was rife in football and can see that things have got better' ... 'At my school there were loads of really good Asian players. To get more Asian players in the game would be good. The talent is there' ... 'Racism seemed to have been cut out of the game, but recently I've heard things and seen things I don't like. We need to kick this stuff out' ... 'For me this campaign is very important, because racism is a big problem, not just in football but in life'. These comments from professional footballers and managers are taken from materials for schools prepared by the Kick It Out campaign.

Initial teacher training rarely covers teaching about racism. However, once they are in school it often falls to committed teachers who have had no specialist training in teaching about racism to do so as part of the PSHE or citizenship education programmes. Organisations such as Kick It Out, the Kick Racism out of Football campaign, produce materials for schools with projects, activities and lessons plans which are motivating to pupils, and which give guidelines on how to teach them. The range of activities includes some which are related to football and others which are not. They can be used by the specialist and the non-specialist teacher, and enjoyed both by pupils who follow football and by those who have no interest in it.

This chapter describes examples of material adapted from the Kick It Out packs for schools. They include three classroom activities based on football, and a whole-school project. They are quoted here with kind permission of Kick It Out. The full packs including worksheets can be obtained from the organisation.

Three classroom activities

These activities harness the motivation that football brings, are based on reality and require students to think about racism, its damaging effects and what actions they might take themselves. They foster empathy and promote reflection on role models. They make the link from football to school.

Facing racism in football and school

To start this activity pupils are told that many black players who played in Britain, particularly during the 1970s and 80s faced abuse from the crowds because of the colour of their skin. This abuse took many forms and included monkey chanting and throwing bananas onto the pitch. Recently there have been several high profile cases when the England team have played overseas. The game between England and Spain in Madrid 2004, for example, gained huge media attention because of the racist abuse hurled at certain England players.

■ Teachers organise a class discussion about how those players would have felt, also how their white team mates might have felt. They could do this in role.

■ Pupils are asked to carry out a mock interview with one of the black players who played in the game about their experiences that night. This activity lends itself to pairs, small group or classroom working. Pupils should be given preparation time to think about the effect on the black players, and to plan sensitive questions. It can be a purely oral activity, or can be written up as a magazine or fanzine interview.

■ Having thought about the effects of racism in football, what would pupils do if they faced racism at school directed at themselves or someone else? In this activity pupils consider their own roles and responsibilities for ensuring their school is free from racism. It is important that they are empowered to believe they all have a responsibility to address this issue, whatever their background. Classes can come up with their own code of conduct. They might present this to their school council or their headteacher, with a view to it being adopted or adapted as a school code of conduct.

■ Much of the racist activity from fans at football matches has been carried out by young people, so young people would have expert advice and ideas about what to do about it. Imagining the time of the World Cup, pupils could be asked to advise the England football authorities about what they should say to fans going abroad to support the England team. They can do this as a class activity or in groups. It can be in the format of a letter to the Football Association, a leaflet or poster for fans, a 10 minute TV programme or a power-point presentation on what should be done. The class may want to actually send the letter and leaflet to the Football Association.

Wall of heroes

■ A Kick it Out football wall of heroes can be prepared. Teachers identify a large wallspace in the classroom, or use a screen, then cover the space with sugar paper. Over the football season, the class builds up a collage of pictures and words. They are invited to bring in photographs of their heroes, and paste them onto the 'wall'. They also paste up quotations using the antiracist football websites to help them, and are invited to write their own words or poems to add to the wall. Women footballers and managers should not be forgotten. At the end of the season a powerful class statement in words and pictures will have been produced. If a competition such as the World Cup or the European Cup is taking place, the wall can be built up for the period of the competition.

■ Themed walls of heroes can be prepared. The wall is prepared as in the activity above, but the theme is heroes who have made a stand against racism (Nelson Mandela, Martin Luther King, Desmond Tutu). Instead or as well, the heroes can be from particular spheres of activity, for example scientists, authors, poets and peacemakers. These walls could also draw on heroes from popular culture, such as the music industry.

Statements about racism in football

■ This is an individual, group or school activity. Pupils are given a set of statements on racism in football made by football icons, and a separate list of those who made them. The task is for individuals or groups to match each statement to the person who made it.

Statements such as the following can be used.

- Football authorities can never relax if the evil of racism in football is to be eradicated. (UEFA Chief Executive Lars-Christer Olsson)

- There is a need for concerted action and an urgency for more severe measures to be adopted in order to kick this evil out of the beautiful game. (FIFA President Joseph S. Blatter)

- My father is black. So I would get racist taunts in school. As soon as you experience it, don't be scared to speak to someone. Because it is scary if you are getting bullied or the person that is bullying you finds out that you told on them. But you need to address it straight away. (Ryan Giggs)

- I'm lucky because as a white person, I've never experienced the kind of racism some suffer. (Warren Barton)

- Their talent will show and people will look beyond the colour of their skin. One Asian player will force their way through and the rest will follow. (Sol Campbell)

- Racism seemed to have been cut out of the game, but recently I've heard things and seen things I don't like. We need to kick this stuff out. (David Beckham)

- As a coach, I never think about the colour of a player's skin. What you're looking for is their abilities and qualities as a footballer and a person. (Sven Goran Eriksson, England Manager)

- Prejudice and racism in any part of life is not acceptable, and football should be no different. (Jose Mourinho)

- The more knowledge that people have of different cultures, the more understanding you can be, for example, during Ramadan, it is important to appreciate about fasting. (Rio Ferdinand)

- As a kid it affects your whole life. Talk to your parents or a teacher. It can affect your school work. (Ryan Giggs)

- For me this campaign is very important, because racism is a big problem, not just in football but in life. (Djibril Cisse)

- If you're being bullied, to get it stopped, go to your teacher, parent or another adult you trust and tell them what's happening. No one in the world should be able to racially abuse another human being. It's out of order. (Sol Campbell)

Teachers and pupils can research quotations such as these and collect additional ones. Useful websites include those of KIO (http://www.kickitout. org), UEFA (http://www.uefagames.com) and Show Racism the Red Card (http://www.srtrc.org).

Individual pupils or groups are also asked to make statements of their own about racism. Finally the individuals or groups can share their own state-ments in a class discussion. These can be displayed on the wall, or the class could be asked to agree a class statement to be displayed on the wall.

A whole-school or whole-year group project
Overview

■ This project reinforces the importance, mentioned throughout this book, of involving children and young people in policy making and producing guidelines. It is a driver for whole school change, and is likely to take at least one term to complete, and more if there is wide involvement and consultation. At best there is involvement of the whole school community. Because this project can lead to funda-mental change it is described here in detail.

■ Aspects of this substantial project contribute to KS1, KS2, KS3 and KS4 curricula in art and design, citizenship, design technology, English, ICT, mathematics, PSHE. Overall it follows recommenda-tions of children and young people's participation in Every Child Matters and the Race Relations Amendment Act.

■ The project is overseen by teachers, but is carried out in a democratic way with the pupils taking leadership roles.

■ It is suggested that preferably this is a project for whole-school in-volvement, or for whole year groups to do. If the school has a school council, the project can be led from there.

Aims and intended outcomes

The aims are for pupils to consider the school environment they want to learn in, and to prepare advice for their peers and the school community on ways to achieve it. The intended outcomes are:

■ pupils gain an understanding about the damaging effects of racism and bullying on the targets, the bullies and the whole school com-munity

■ they consider their own and other pupils' experiences and feelings

■ they have the opportunity of finding their own solutions

■ a final document or a set of documents is produced which are relevant to the pupils and contain a code of conduct

■ the final document is useful to the whole school community – pupils, staff, parents, governors – and can be used to inform policy and strategy

■ the process of carrying out this project will have a positive effect on the school ethos

■ pupils gain in confidence and improve their attainment in a range of national curriculum subjects

Context

■ The project takes account of the voices of children as experts, knowing what happens in school, knowing how to talk to their peers and wanting to learn in a peaceful, inclusive environment free from bullying and racism.

■ Similar work has been done with pupils aged from 5 to 18, from mainstream and special schools, and has been very successful. Even the youngest children had powerful and perceptive contributions to make.

■ The kind of advice which comes out of the project will have different emphases in schools in diverse city areas and schools in mainly white areas, and this makes the project even more valuable. It allows schools to customise their policies and strategies.

Organisation

Although the details of how the project progresses will be different in every school, there are some broad steps which will be taken whichever model is chosen.

■ The project begins with the staff involved agreeing what they want to come out of it, and how they will organise it.

■ Staff involved inform the rest of the school staff. They may also wish to inform parents and governors.

■ The project is introduced to the pupils in the appropriate groupings (eg classes, school council, year group.) It is made clear to pupils that most of them are kind, caring and respectful of each other, but that the school takes a strong stand against racism of any sort and they are asking pupils to help them prepare advice. In this first session pupils brainstorm what kind of school they want to learn in.

■ Pupils are asked to go away on a fact-finding mission, to research the experiences of pupils in the school in respect of racism. They might do this through discussion in class, circle time, or designing questionnaires. This will vary considerably according to the age of the pupils.

■ Findings of the initial research phase are discussed in individual classes. From the outset the teacher will need to stress that these sessions are absolutely confidential, and that pupils are expected to respect and support each other. Classes brainstorm what makes up racism, and come to their own definition and understanding of it. This will be refined later. If there is a school council, the representatives take the information back to it. Notes are taken of what pupils are saying, and this may be best done on a flipchart and typed up later. Some pupils may feel safe enough to give sensitive and painful information and if so they must be supported. Pupils are asked to think about what might be included in their advice and bring ideas to the next session.

■ At the next session, pupils decide on a framework for the advice and what sections they want to see included. The school council or, if there isn't one, the staff make a synthesis of the suggestions and prepare a final framework. The work of writing the sections is allocated to the classes involved. It is valuable to have a document written by pupils in their own language register so the teachers should only edit it for spelling and clarity.

■ Some examples of how the work might be allocated to classes follow. Pupils may prepare

   ☐ advice for peers in their own key stage

   ☐ advice on different issues

   ☐ advice to school staff about how they would like the staff to support them

   ☐ a list of what staff have done which they value as effective

   ☐ a code of conduct for themselves

   ☐ different advice for targets, bullies and witnesses

☐ information about the duty to record and report racist incidents, and the school procedures

☐ an answer to the question 'What kind of school do we want to learn in?'

☐ a definition of racism, based on the initial brainstorm

Outcomes and presentation

The final product is a school publication or set of small publications. It will include guidelines, but can be worked up to produce a school policy on combating racism.

The school will decide how it is to be used and disseminated, depending on the technology and funding available. Every pupil and all staff and governors should have access to it, and parents should be aware of it. Pupils might also want to present their views by making presentations, posters, video programmes or plays, or in other ways.

General notes

■ This project is best carried out as a whole-school project. For that to happen it requires the agreement of all staff.

■ As a whole-school project, it can be led through the school council. Those which do not have one will need a steering group of staff.

■ It contains activities which go across several curriculum areas and attainment targets. So in a **secondary school** the staff could decide to work together in various ways which suit them. For example, the discussion and decision could take place either in tutorial periods or in PSHE or citizenship education classes. The art and design, design technology, English and mathematics departments could be linked into the project, because activities could be carried out to meet attainment targets in all these subjects.

■ If only one key stage or one year group is involved, similar organisation will be required.

■ Organising the project as two separate projects for key stages 3 and 4 and put together at the end will be more manageable in a big high school.

■ In the **primary school** the class teachers will have more flexibility in how they organise the project as a curriculum activity. Even the youngest pupils have something to contribute, and should be involved. It is useful to have pupils at key stages 1 and 2 write in their own language register.

Supporting pupils

■ The issues will differ in schools in multiethnic urban areas and in mainly white areas. In all cases it is important to support pupils who may have been targets of racism and who are vulnerable. They should be listened to sensitively and their experiences taken seriously. This is all the more important in schools in which such pupils are few and isolated.

■ Carrying out such a project may give rise to situations or comments in the classroom and also the staffroom which are difficult and require sensitivity to deal with.

Concluding note

'If you're being bullied, to get it stopped, go to your teacher, parent or another adult you trust and tell them what's happening. No one in the world should be able to racially abuse another human being. It's out of order.' This was the advice to children and young people from football icon Sol Campbell, quoted by Kick It Out. Comments such as these show the potential of popular culture as a vehicle for antiracism. So many young people are passionately interested in football – the fortunes of their local or favourite team, who represents their country in the national team, football as aspect of global culture, football as a symbol of the importance of rules and accepting referees' decisions, and – not least – football as a frequent recreational activity. It makes good sense in schools to capitalise on young people's passions, interests and heroes.

Other areas of popular culture provide teachers with motivational hooks to catch the interest of their pupils. Rugby and cricket, for example, have organisations making strong statements against racism in their sports. The music industry organises mass festivals with antiracist themes. All provide role models for children and young people and give out messages to stand up against racism and bullying. Popular writers such as Benjamin Zephaniah and Malorie Blackman offer antiracist messages for teachers to use as a starting point for introducing the topic of racism into their classrooms. The next chapter looks at the use of theatre to teach against racism in the classroom, and considers forum theatre as an agent of individual and collective change.

9

Changed me completely into a new person
From bystander to active citizen

Ally is black and was born in Manchester. Recently she moved to a rural school in Cumbria, where she is subject to racist bullying. Teachers at the school are unable, or perhaps unwilling, to intervene at all constructively and the story ends sadly for all concerned.

Ally is the principal character in a piece of forum theatre (Knowles and Ridley, 2006:58-60) and the show is performed twice. During the second performance, members of the audience – known now as spectActors – are invited to intervene whenever they think one of the characters has an opportunity to do something that will put a stop to the bullying and prevent it from occurring again. The spectActor can explain their point by rehearsing the reality they are proposing, for example by temporarily replacing a character and showing what they think the protagonist should have done. The actors improvise back, in character, and the audience decides whether the intervention was successful. In this way they not only change the outcome of the play but also display and rehearse the moral courage and resolution of citizens, who are active, not passive and indifferent. At best, they are engaged in what was described in chapter 4 as transformative justice. Primary school children who have seen the play have written:

> After watching the play, I feel a better person and I feel as if it has changed me completely into a new person and I will never say anything about other people that is racist again.
>
> I am being very honest. I did used to sometimes say things but I didn't realise what I was saying until I thought about what I had done and then I would feel so guilty that I would go to my room for a bit. But after watching the play I really felt as if I

was black or Asian and I knew what it was to get picked on for my colour or religion so I think that the play really helps you to know what a black person might feel like'

After the play I realised that calling black people names that are nasty can really upset the person's feelings inside their body so from now on I will never call black people nasty names again, 'cause I know now how much pain they get.

I feel a bit more aware of what things you can say to be racist and how it affects people in different ways and how people can react.

At the beginning I thought that the character Billy [who leads the racist taunting] was quite funny but through the play I didn't because he started going too far and hurting. I never knew racism could be so rough and hurtful. I very much enjoyed the play though.

The concept of forum theatre was developed by Brazilian theatre director Augusto Boal. He was much influenced by Brazilian educator Paulo Freire, whose best known book is *Pedagogy of the Oppressed*. In his approach to theatrical performance and to the role of theatre in relation to social justice, Boal was influenced by the German dramatist Bertolt Brecht.

A forum theatre presentation typically portrays a situation in which an individual or community is a victim of injustice. From time to time the action on stage is stopped and members of the audience are invited to make suggestions about how the unjust situation should be challenged. Typically they make the suggestions directly to the actors, the actors remaining in role. The actors then take up the audience's suggestions and alter the story accordingly. Nevertheless, the presentation usually ends on a note of uncertainty and apparent defeat. It is up to the audience to think through the practical implications, not only for themselves as individuals but also for the community to which they belong.

Boal (1992:230) mantained that the purpose of forum theatre is in the first instance to achieve a good debate rather than a good solution – a good debate being one in which people engage not only with their minds but also with empathy and emotional solidarity towards those who suffer from injustice, and with resolve to create better and fairer systems and relationships. The process of continually stopping the action and inviting the audience to interact with the characters means that the audience cannot just sit back passively. Boal and Brecht saw a connection between passivity in front of a stage and passivity in the face of real events and situations. According to their theory, if audiences are prevented from being passive when they observe imaginary events, they are less likely to be passive in their dealings with real situations.

Forum theatre can valuably involve puppets instead of live actors. UNICEF education department, for example, has devised a puppet show about a cat and a fox. The cat and his father run the only shop in the forest. They refuse to serve the fox, on the grounds that foxes are 'Pointies' and they refer to foxes with a stream of negative stereotypes. The son eventually changes his views, however, whereas his father remains bigoted to the end (Barton and Schamroth, 2004).

With puppets, as with live actors, preparation and follow-up both have to be carefully designed. The UNICEF team start a session with the children making statues representing a moment in their school lives when they felt good about themselves. The children suggest words which best describe these positive feelings and these are recorded on a chart. Next, they make statues representing moments at school that were negative and the words they use to describe their feelings are also written on the chart. The lists of words become points of reference for reflections and discussions about the cat and the fox. The follow-up may include exploring *Zaynab's Story* by Lenford Anthony White, the story of Rosa Parks and the Montgomery Bus Boycott, poems by Langston Hughes, and Martin Luther King's *I Have a Dream*.

When Derbyshire County Council planned its responses to the Stephen Lawrence Inquiry report it commissioned Actorshop, a forum theatre company based in London, to enact a story about racist incidents in schools and the response of the staff. The play was intended for audiences of teachers, administrative staff, mid-day supervisors and school governors but was also performed for pupils. An extended summary of the action (Box 9.1) shows the many opportunities the play provides for thoughtful, vigorous and constructive discussion. It can have a powerful impact on not just individuals but whole school communities.

Box 9.1: A forum theatre storyline

The principal characters are two Year 6 pupils, Patricia, who is of mixed heritage, and Kerry, who is white. There are three other characters, all of them white: Derek Brown and James Price, respectively the head and a class teacher at the school attended by Patricia and Kerry, and Patricia's mother Sue. Patricia's father is black and she is the only pupil in the school who is not white. The first example of racism in the story arises shortly before an inter-school netball match. In the changing room a member of the opposing team sees Patricia and says, 'Oh, I thought we'd come to play netball, not to watch Planet of the Apes.' Patricia is distressed by the insult, particularly since it is greeted by sniggers from members of her own team rather than

---

by support for her. The insults and sniggers continue and in desperation she throws a ball hard into her tormentor's face, causing a copious nose bleed.

Patricia's teacher, James, sees the injured girl but has no idea why Patricia attacked her. He insists angrily that she apologise and refuses to listen to anything she tries to say by way of explanation. He also brushes off Kerry when she comes to her friend's defence. Patricia storms off home ('I'm sick of this stupid school') without playing in the match. Next day, Patricia is in additional trouble because she went home without permission. James declares she must apologise in writing to the other school. She again refuses. There appears to be a total impasse but Kerry enters and manages to get James to listen to a full account of what actually happened. He realises there was provocation and that he was too hasty in his judgement. Kerry also tells him that Pat and her mother frequently experience racism in the neighbourhood where they live. He agrees to go and visit them at their home.

When James visits them a few days later he is tongue-tied and awkward and gives no more than a garbled account of what happened. Sue jumps to the conclusion that Patricia has let her down by engaging in unprovoked violence and for a moment poor Patricia is utterly desolate and alone. But her mother is loving and attentive and quickly listens and understands, and gives her daughter a powerful sense of moral support and solidarity. James goes to see the headteacher, Derek Brown, to tell him about the racism frequently experienced by Sue and her mother in the school's neighbourhood, and to tell him that Pat was provoked by racist insults. The head, however, is far more interested in a broken handbell he is examining. ('I don't want to have to get a new bell, James, I really don't.') He acknowledges he knows Patricia – 'that coloured kid' – but says the racism she has been subjected to isn't important so far as he is concerned, since she will be transferring to secondary school in a few months time. He reluctantly agrees, however, that James should organise an entertainment for parents on the theme of celebrating cultural diversity.

The head mutters also that James is welcome to convene a working party, if he would like to, to produce a school policy on race equality. 'I suppose it wouldn't be a bad idea to have a policy, come to think of it,' he adds. 'We're probably going to get other coloured kids in the future. The Home Secretary says schools like ours are in danger of being swamped by asylum-seekers and Muslims and people like that.'

The entertainment takes place a few weeks later and Pat is the star, appearing in it both as an African dancer and as an Indian dancer. James and the head congratulate her on her fine performances. Her mother approaches and the two teachers turn to her and remark she must be very proud of her daughter. 'Yes,' says Sue, 'she's quite good for a nigger, isn't she? Though mind you, all niggers are pretty good at dancing, they have a natural sense of rhythm.' It transpires quickly that she is quoting remarks she heard around her from other parents during the show. Sue begins to sob as she says she and Patricia have been let down by the school and that she believes her precious daughter has no future, anyway in this part of England. 'Will at least the secondary school she's moving to be the right place for her?' she asks. James and the head have no idea. They stand there speechless. Sue continues to sob, uncontrollably.

After the play the actors remain in role in order to take questions from the audience. Then members of the audience talk about their most vivid memories of the play. At one performance these included the following:

- when Patricia felt she was totally alone, deserted even by her own mother

- but then the expression of Sue's love for her daughter a few seconds later and her determination to stand by her

- Sue's use of the word nigger and the devastating shock it caused the audience

- the headteacher fidgeting with a bell when he should have been giving James his full attention

- shivers through the audience when the head referred to 'that coloured kid' and showed (for example by his casual endorsement of an infamous remark by the then Home Secretary) how ignorant and insensitive he was

- the head giving no support or guidance to the class teacher

- the class teacher jumping to a conclusion and refusing to listen to Patricia's story

- James's inability to use the word racism until pressed (repeatedly!) by the audience to do so

- later, James's pain when he realises he doesn't have an easy answer and has to re-think aspects of his personal and professional identity

- Patricia's mounting frustration when the teacher won't listen to her

- that Patricia and her mum are so accustomed to having to put up with racism in their neighbourhood

Last not least, the most powerful, heart-stopping memories included Kerry defending her friend Pat to the hilt, and her account of what adults in her family say when she challenges them about racism:

> 'They go 'yeah, yeah, yeah', they say I'm just a kid, which I am, but I know stuff they don't.'

An active citizen indeed, not a bystander.

It is not only the audience that benefits from forum theatre. The actors also learn a great deal – they too may have life-changing experiences. An all-white team of actors was interviewed about what they had gained from researching, rehearsing and performing a piece about racist bullying in schools in Wiltshire (Carroll, 2004) and these were some of their comments:

> It has been such a worthwhile project because it has allowed me to grow as a person and also to give something of myself in the service of something important, which I now feel passionate about.

We have been on a long journey of discovery together. I am sure the process will continue. Without doubt it is necessary to keep challenging the racist attitudes, both open and hidden.

Entering the role of victim has been very revealing. It's a devastating place to be in, although I don't feel I've been anywhere near to where discrimination can really take someone.

It is extremely rewarding to be part of a project that has challenged me on a personal and creative way. We are all responsible in the fight against racism.

All schools need to create a climate where racism comes out from under the carpet and where potential and current victims of racism and white peers feel it is worthwhile doing something positive about it.

Actor and audience

Much bullying in schools, as mentioned in chapter 3, has the characteristics of a performance, with actors speaking or improvising lines based on a standard script ('go back where you came from' or whatever) and an audience of passive but approving bystanders already broadly familiar with the story unfolding before their eyes. The performance was represented schematically in figure 3.1, and is shown on the book's cover. The educational task is to transform bystanders into active citizens – people who will come to the defence and aid of whoever is cast as victim, and will stand up to whoever is taking or has been allotted the role of ringleader or henchperson; and who will play a part in restoring the community that has been harmed or broken. Forum theatre, which dissolves conventional proscenium-arch boundaries between audiences, actors, scriptwriters, stagehands and directors, clearly has the potential to move pupils from the stalls to centre-stage and, more importantly, to enable them to take and practise the role of active citizen.

All four of the pieces of forum theatre referred to – from Cumbria, Dorset, Derbyshire and Wiltshire – involved visitors to a school who were mostly professional or near-professional actors. So the events were expensive. The principles underlying forum theatre, however, are all present in activities known variously and loosely as process drama, drama-as-education, dramatic inquiry and teacher-in-role (Braverman, 2002; Edmiston, 2008; Hennessy, 2007; Taylor and Warner, 2006; Winston, 1998). Such activities are not primarily concerned with imparting information to individuals, as is the case with much of education, but focus primarily on 'how people identify with others, get along with others in social communities and cultures, learn to take action to influence how people use power' and 'how people can know what they do is right' (Edmiston, 2008:42). Through drama, writes Joe Winston, the school classroom can become a 'communal, public stage where ... virtues can be problematised, played with, subverted, reframed, or brought into conflict with one another. Through generating moral engagement and active inquiry, drama can deepen a child's sensitivity to and understanding of the complexities of the moral life' (Winston, 1998:176).

Process drama techniques can be used with many of the topics covered in this book, for example the stories about racism in football in chapter 8, and stories in the media discussed in chapter 10. Here are possible scenarios relating to everyday life at school:

- Ahmed and Salma seem to have become depressed and withdrawn and to be avoiding people in the playground. Then Jenny comes to school and says she saw them in the supermarket queue with their mother at the weekend, and two women were shouting at their mother 'You lot should get back home. You're terrorists, we don't want your sort here.'

- At the lunch table David tells an Irish joke. Mary says she doesn't like it because it stereotypes all Irish people as stupid, but David says 'I didn't mean anything, and everybody laughed anyway. You are too sensitive.'

- Jerry's gang is the most powerful gang in the year. Everyone wants to be in it and Steve is really glad to be accepted into it and he is proud of the status he gets as a member. Only white boys can be in the gang, and they use racist language about boys from other backgrounds. After a while Steve begins to feel uncomfortable about this and wants to get out of the gang. He doesn't know how.

- Said and Amin love playing football. Both very good and are picked for the school team. They never miss team practice every Wednesday after school. When the team practice day is changed to Friday, however, they apologise and say they will have to resign from the team, explaining to the PE teacher they can't stay after school on Fridays because they go to the mosque.

Concluding note

'Good drama for me,' wrote theatre critic Kenneth Tynan, 'is made up of the thoughts, the words and the gestures that are wrung from human beings on their way to, or in, or emerging from, a state of desperation' (Tynan, 1957). He was referring to the professional theatre, but could also have had in mind –

for example – the story from Derbyshire outlined above, the one featuring Patricia and her mother Sue and friend Kerry, that ended with Sue's desperation as she contemplated a hopeless future in white Britain. Within the story itself no one emerged from a state of desperation. But from the theatrical performance and its discussion, hope did emerge, crystallised on behalf of the audience by some words of the active citizen Kerry: They go 'yeah, yeah, yeah', they say I'm just a kid, which I am, but I know stuff they don't.'

One of the duties of active citizens is to keep themselves informed about what is going on in the world. They need, therefore, to read newspapers, watch telly, surf the internet. But what are the pictures of the world they meet there? How do they decide which pictures are more or less true, and which more or less false? These are essential questions for any teacher intending to prevent racism and value cultural diversity through the school curriculum. They are the central questions of the next chapter.

10

Pictures of the world in the mind's eye
Images and narratives in the media

'Imagine a typical American,' writes a social studies specialist in one of the first books ever published on media studies in schools, 'who has just boarded the 8.02 am bus on his way to work. His favourite newspaper is under his arm as he walks down the aisle, sits down, opens the paper and begins to read' (Nesbitt, 1971:5). The author continues: 'There is far more to this common-place encounter of a man and his newspaper than meets the eye.' He proceeds to explain:

> On the one hand, the newspaper represents the end product of an elaborate chain of activities involving news gathering, transmission and processing by humans and machines. On the other hand, our man on the bus is the product of his experiences – recent and remote, transitory and permanent – which influence what the newspaper means to him... Any individual selects, distorts, remembers, understands, agrees with or disagrees with what he reads in the light of his individual experiences ... The messages on the page ... are processed to make sense according to the pictures of the world already in the mind's eye.

The media themselves – including movies, computer games, comics, video clips, music, radio phone-in programmes, websites and the blogosphere – are a major source of 'pictures of the world already in the mind's eye'. So are generations of school textbooks. In relation to the themes and concerns of this book, what pictures in the mind's eye are daily reflected and reinforced in the media? Do they reflect and affirm the identities and experiences of all pupils, or do they leave some of them invisible, or project images that negative and demeaning? Do the pictures hinder or help schools to deal with bullying around racism, culture and religion? In so far as they are a hindrance, what can schools appropriately and responsibly do to counteract them? These are the key questions addressed in this chapter.

In his ground-breaking study of the American press in the early twentieth century the commentator Walter Lippmann (1922, cited in Nesbitt, 1971:5) wrote:

> It is because they are compelled to act without a reliable picture of the world that governments, schools, newspapers and churches make such small headway against the more obvious failings of democracy, against violent prejudice, apathy, preference for the curious trivial as against the dull important, and the hunger for sideshows and three-legged calves.

Three essential educational tasks are evoked here: a) learners in schools need to be equipped with pictures of the world that are reliable, so that they make or support sound judgments and decisions at times of stress, uncertainty and conflict; b) the purpose is to make headway against the more obvious failings of democracy, and on the contrary to support and strengthen agreed procedures of deliberation, dialogue and debate; and c) teachers have to teach engagingly and excitingly about 'the dull important' even though there is widespread preference for 'the curious trivial', symbolised by sideshows and three-legged calves.

These tasks involve equipping learners to understand underlying issues and historical contexts that the Glasgow University Media Group found in their study of the effect of TV news. TV viewers who felt they were watching 'an incomprehensible and irresolvable litany of death and suffering', switched channels or simply walked away from their screens. The researchers quoted a student who commented that the news 'never explains it so I don't see the point in watching it – I just turn it off and just go and make a cup of tea or something. I don't like watching it when I don't understand what's going on' (Philo and Berry, 2004:240). Such passivity is the hallmark of a bystander as distinct from an active citizen.

If pupils are to be empowered to be active citizens in relation to the media, and potentially therefore to be active in challenging racist behaviour and bullying in their own school, they need to engage in classroom activities and projects such as the following:

- They are given a list of questions to ask about a news story on TV or in a paper, and use these with regard to a specific cutting, or item on a website, or clip of film. Instead or as well, they use the same list to compare and contrast coverage of a particular story as presented on the website of BBC News and the website of a tabloid paper. On the basis of their analysis, they draft an imaginary letter to the editors or to the Press Complaints Commission. If the item is recent, they write such a letter for real. There is a specimen list of questions in box 10.1, adapted from a book for teachers about Muslim perspectives on citizenship education (Imran and Miskell, 2004).

■ They consider some news stories about Islam in Britain and Islam in the world, and whether the stories show 'the West' and Islam as locked in inevitable conflict (a 'clash of civilisations') or whether there can on the contrary be partnership and cooperation. On the basis of their reflections and conclusions they write real or imaginary letters to the local and national media and to local councillors and their constituency MP.

■ They create their own newspaper-style or TV-style reports, based on real or imaginary events in their own school. In chapter 4 (box 4.1) there was a collection of episodes in school life that raise issues about prejudice and racism. Any one of these can be developed into a news story and pupils have then to grapple with the technical and ethical questions that are necessarily involved in how the story is to be presented.

■ They sort through ten or so snippets of news, or about ten real or imaginary press releases, and imagine themselves to be an editorial team whose task is to put the items in a sequence and to allocate space and time for each. It is instructive if each group adopts the stance of a specific paper or TV channel.

■ They study a set of TV or magazine advertisements, considering them both as windows and as mirrors. Are they themselves reflected in them? How are identities and communities in modern society depicted? Are certain identities and communities not represented at all?

■ They monitor their own TV viewing for a week, noting the numbers of people they see who are of the same ethnicity as themselves, and the contexts (for example whether positive or negative) in which they are seen.

■ They compare and contrast images and stories in mainstream papers with images and stories in papers such as *Asian Times, Muslim News, New Nation* and *The Voice.*

■ They study the depiction of certain communities, for example British Muslims, people seeking asylum, African-Caribbean people and Gypsies and Travellers.

Box

What is fact and what is interpretation?

Can you distinguish the facts whose accuracy can be readily checked from statements of opinion and interpretation?

What language is used?

Are words neutral or are they emotive and loaded? For example, how are words such as *freedom-fighter*, *terrorist* and *insurgent* used? Or *invasion* and *liberation*, and *conservative* and *fundamentalist*? How does the report use the word *say*, implying that someone is telling the truth, and the word *claim*, implying that someone may not be? What choice is made between *Third World* and *Global South*?

Is the account balanced?

Is more than one point of view reported, and is each different point of view presented fairly and neutrally?

Complexity and uncertainty

When points of view are reported is it acknowledged that the people quoted are in certain respects uncertain, both in their perceptions of what actually happened and in their interpretations and opinions?

Quotations

Who is directly quoted and how are they referred to? For example, are they said to be 'experts', 'professionals' or 'representatives'? How much information is given about who they are? Does it sometimes happen that someone is quoted anonymously, and could the quotation therefore be fictitious?

Background

Reporters and newscasters frequently go for 'bang bang' items with immediate and attention-grabbing impact rather than provide 'explainers', giving information about the general context and historical background. What is the balance in the report you are looking at between explainers on the one hand and immediate facts on the other?

Cause and effect

Reports sometimes run two items together with words such as *following, later, subsequently, previously*. When they use such words, they do not actually say that there is a causal connection between the events but they do imply it. Is this apparent in the report you are studying?

Motivations

Are words used which imply how someone is motivated and could it be that they are misleading? For example, the phrases *Muslim terrorist* and *Islamic terrorist* are frequently used, but the term *Christian terrorist* in reports from Northern Ireland have seldom if ever been used.

> **Freedom to make up one's mind**
> This is one of the most important questions of all. News channels claim to distinguish between providing facts and providing interpretations. But do they in fact do this? Are you confident that you can make up your own mind on the basis of what is reported, or can you see that you are being subtly – or perhaps unsubtly – led to adopt a particular point of view?
>
> **What are the assumptions about the audience?**
> Who does the reporter think they are talking to? That is, what knowledge and understanding do they assume the audience to have, and what predispositions and expectations?
>
> *Source: adapted from Imran and Maskell, 2003*

Narratives

The West's war against terror, wrote the defence correspondent of the *Daily Telegraph* in October 2001, 'belongs within the much larger spectrum of a far older conflict between settled, creative productive Westerners and predatory, destructive Orientals.' On 11 September, he said, 'the Oriental tradition ... returned in an absolutely traditional form. Arabs, appearing suddenly out of empty space like their desert raider ancestors, assaulted the heartlands of Western power, in a terrifying surprise raid.' His words were a vivid and dramatic summary of the way the Western media both reflected and shaped how the events of 9/11 were seen. They also illustrated the way in which news stories in the media are frequently embedded in an overall narrative.

A narrative seeks to explain patterns of cause and effect, and who or what is to blame. It provides a stock of metaphors, analogies and vivid imagery, as in the extract about 9/11 cited above, and a recurring concern is to establish – again, as in the example cited above – the distinctive features of 'us' and 'them', self and other, insider and outsider, allies and enemies, victims and aggressors, those who 'really' belong in one's own society or civilisation and those who do not. In relation to us and them, Table 10.1 suggests that narratives differ from each other on a continuum from closed to open and that the five principal components of a narrative are to do with uniformity/diversity, difference/similarity, inferiority/equality, threat/trust and conflict/cooperation. The table as it stands is highly abstract. It can readily be unpacked, however, in considerations of particular news stories in the media.

'Pupils need to be able to interpret reports,' argues a DfES consultation paper, 'and develop skills to interrogate and make judgements about how their meaning is constructed and conveyed. While different localities may have

Table 10.1: VIEWS OF US AND THEM

Points of contrast	Closed narratives	Open narratives
Uniformity/diversity	They are all much the same	There is great diversity amongst them
Difference/similarity	They are significantly different from us	There are many commonalities between them and us
Inferiority/equality	They are morally and culturally inferior to us	There is both good and bad everywhere – both in them and us
Threat/trust	They are a threat to us	There are both real and perceived threats on both sides
Conflict/cooperation	There is no possibility of them and us living and working cooperatively together.	It is both possible and urgent that they and we should work together on solving or managing shared problems and on building mutual confidence

Source: adapted from Insted Consultancy for the Greater London Authority 2007

different contexts, the media, especially the press and TV, are universally available and afford all pupils opportunities to explore diversity and its representations. Critical literacy is crucial' (Ajegbo, 2007:69). It continues by stressing the role and responsibility of schools in this respect:

> If you are white, for example, living in a white area, how do you relate what you see on the television to your idea of being British and the nature of British society? If you are black, how do you interpret programmes on AIDs and famine in Africa, or inner city issues in America? If you are Muslim, how do you cope with the barrage of media images about terrorism or the veil? Schools must play their part in re-capturing the middle ground for groups who are misrepresented.

A similar emphasis on the importance of media literacy in combating racism has been made internationally (Office for Democratic Institutions and Human Rights, 2007). The Association for Media Literacy, based in Canada, identifies ten key concepts underlying the theoretical base for all media literacy programmes and gives teachers a common language and framework for discussion. In summary, the concepts are as follows.

■ All media are constructions. When analysing a media text consider how the message is constructed and how well it represents reality.

■ Each person interprets messages in their own way. Your interpretation will reflect your age, culture, life experience, gender, values and interests. How might others understand the same text differently?

■ The media have commercial interests. Most media are created for profit and advertising is generally the biggest source of revenue. When analysing a media text, consider: who created this and why. Who profits if the message is accepted? Who may be disadvantaged?

■ The media contain ideological messages. Producers have their own beliefs, values, opinions and biases which can influence what gets told and how it is told. What lifestyles, values and points of view are represented in or omitted from a message? What does a message say about the nature of the good life, the virtue of consumerism, the role of women, the acceptance of authority, cultural and ethnic diversity, and patriotism and national identity?

■ Each medium has its own language, style, techniques, codes, conventions and aesthetics. When analysing a media text, consider the techniques that are used and why. This enables you not only to decode and understand media texts but also to enjoy the unique aesthetic form of each. Your enjoyment of media is enhanced by an awareness of the ways in which pleasing forms and effects are created.

■ There are commercial implications. Ninety per cent of the world's newspapers, magazines, television stations, films and computer software companies are owned by seven corporate conglomerates. Issues of ownership and control are of vital importance at a time when there are more choices but fewer voices.

■ There are social and political implications. A function of the mass media is to legitimise, endorse and reinforce certain societal values and attitudes, and certain modes of conducting debates about controversial issues, locally, nationally and globally.

■ Form and content are closely related. In certain respects, the medium is the message. That is, each medium has its own special grammar and technological bias and codifies reality in unique ways. Different media may report the same event but create different impressions and different messages.

Teaching about racism in the media necessarily involves staff in leading discussions of topics on which society is divided, and on which there is likely to be a wide range of opinions and viewpoints amongst not only the pupils themselves but also amongst their parents. So staff need to agree with each other on how such issues should be handled. The following five principles have been drawn from the DfES materials on bullying around racism, culture and religion (DfES, 2006a:85-90), an international symposium reporting on projects in several different countries (Claire and Holden, 2007), a handbook for teachers on religious education (Gluck Wood, 2007) and advice on teaching emotive and controversial issues in the past (Historical Association, 2007). The DfES guidance draws on publications by the Citizenship Foundation, London, and the Morningside Center for Teaching Social Responsibility, New York.

First, the fundamental educational task is to help pupils think for themselves, and sort out and clarify their emotions and values. They therefore need skills in weighing up evidence, choosing between alternatives, thinking about pros and cons, listening and reflecting before coming to a conclusion, developing empathy for people with whom they disagree, and abiding by rules and conventions of mutual respect and civil argument. So it is often appropriate to turn pupils' questions round – 'What do you think?', 'Why?', 'Have you always thought that?', 'Are there other ways of seeing this?', 'What would count as evidence for or against your point of view?', 'What do you think might cause you to change your mind?'

Second, it is miseducation or even indoctrination to say or imply there is consensus around certain issues when in fact there is not. In national society, as also across world society as a whole, there are substantial differences in values and policies. It can be reassuring rather than alarming or depressing to children and young people to be reminded that their elders are in disagreement with each other about important matters. It may be more important for them to live with differences and uncertainties than to settle for over-simple solutions. Controversy, not only about current issues but also about how to interpret the past, is the lifeblood of democracy. It is important that pupils should recognise and welcome this, instead of being afraid of it.

Third, it is essential to provide a safe environment. Fears of ridicule or of being isolated may make pupils wary about expressing their own views or asking questions or thinking aloud – classroom discussions can be under-heated, rather than too lively. So before hard and conflictual issues are broached and discussed, it is frequently necessary to establish an atmosphere of mutual trust. This may sometimes involve various activities and exercises

106

which are not immediately or directly relevant to the subject-matter under consideration. Also, it involves using techniques such as process drama, listening triads, ranking exercises, imaginative literature, case studies, dilemmas in everyday life, hot-seating, buzzing, communication games, visual material, and so on. It is also valuable if pupils formulate their own rules of procedure and if these are published as a wall poster.

Fourth, it follows that a balance has to be struck between freedom of expression and freedom from threat. Freedom of thought and expression is an important value and should be protected in schools as in wider society. It is crucial in classroom discussions that pupils should be able to think aloud and form ideas and opinions through dialogue, debate and disagreement. Freedom of expression is not, however, an absolute value. For it has to be balanced with the equally important right not to be threatened or abused. In practice, the law of the land often puts the right of a person to live in peace and security higher than the right of another person to express their views in insulting and threatening ways. This is appropriate in schools as well – freedom of expression does not include the right to be threatening and abusive, particularly towards pupils who are especially vulnerable to hate crimes on the streets and to racist taunts and bullying within the school's sphere of influence.

Fifth, there are certain fundamental moral principles enshrined in national law and international human rights standards. It is entirely appropriate for teachers and other adults to assert and stress the values in, for example, the Universal Declaration on Human Rights, or in UK and European anti-discrimination legislation. That said, the educational task is to foster understanding of the principles underlying legislation, and commitment to those principles, and not just inform pupils about what is and is not legally acceptable. It must also be acknowledged there are sometimes legitimate disagreements about what the rights and laws involve in practice, and how competing rights and priorities are to be balanced. If children are to understand the spirit of the law, not just the letter, they need to be initiated into the debates the adult world has conducted over the decades and centuries, not merely be told historical or legal facts.

Concluding note

The media have the potential to help shape accurate and reliable pictures of the world in the minds of their readers and viewers and can help shape habits of critical literacy, dialogue and deliberative democracy. But they also have the potential to obfuscate and spread moral panic, to reinforce inaccurate stereotypes and narratives about 'us' and 'them', and to close down thought and debate. The curriculum in schools should help pupils to examine critically the images and stories they meet they encounter in the press and on TV. Such work is necessarily collective, based on shared responsibility. How to promote and sustain shared responsibility is the subject of the next chapter.

11
The table of shared responsibility
Security and challenge in staff development

'Typically,' said a speaker at a national conference in autumn 2005 on countering racist bullying in schools, 'we think about training in terms of skills, knowledge and understanding. But whenever there's training which involves the element of race, it has to be more than that ... It has to engage hearts and minds, it has to force us to contemplate our humanity, it's got to make us think about love and care and concern and kindness.' She continued:

> We have to acknowledge the guilt that some of our white colleagues feel and the resentment and anger of some of our black colleagues and we've got to come to a position collectively, where we agree that guilt and blame have no place at the dining table of shared responsibility. (Quoted in Richardson, 2006)

This chapter is a reflection on how training sessions and courses for teachers should ideally be structured and patterned, if those challenging and inspiring words are to be heeded. The dining table as a metaphor for people coming together as equals for a shared purpose and a shared future, overcoming but not denying legacies of guilt, blame, resentment and anger, occurs in a famous poem by Langston Hughes about national identity in the United States. The voice in the poem is that of an African American who lives in a white household. 'I am the darker brother,' he says. 'They send me to eat in the kitchen/When company comes.' He then looks ahead to a future when he will be seen and honoured as a full member of society: 'Tomorrow,/I'll be at the table/When company comes/Nobody'll dare/Say to me,/'Eat in the kitchen,'/Then.' He concludes: 'I, too, am America.' Since hearts are to be engaged as well as minds, metaphors and echoes from poetry as well as prose are appropriate, in considerations of inservice training and professional development in the field of race equality.

Objectives

The objectives of staff training in the race equality field were itemised as follows by the Commission on the Future of Multi-Ethnic Britain, drawing on work by Jozimba Panthera (2000: paragraph 20.13, slightly adapted):

- becoming aware of unconscious racism, and owning the feelings of guilt and embarrassment which arise

- recognising that white people were not given a choice of whether or not to internalise racism and therefore do not have to defend themselves from acknowledging that they have been affected by it

- exploring and understanding the experiences, stories and expectations of people who have suffered directly from racism

- developing skills in identifying and challenging racism in the institutions in which one works, and particularly within one's own sphere of responsibility, and in practical planning and action to remove it

- developing cultural literacy – an awareness of problems of misperception and miscommunication in cross-cultural settings, particularly when there is not only cultural difference but also a power differential

- understanding that the alternative to racism is a transformed community of citizens and communities, so developing concepts of human rights, social cohesion, equality and respect for difference.

Chapter 4 outlined the need for a transformative approach to racist bullying, as distinct from an approach that is dismissive, punitive or corrective. When a transformative approach is adopted, an incident of racist bullying is seen as more than just an episode. It is seen also as an epicentre – a signal that there are seismic shifts, contradictions and unresolved conflicts beneath the surface. Thus there is a need not only to deal with the immediate situation but also to tackle long term issues. These are frequently to do with deep-seated feelings and anxieties about the sources of people's sense of identity and self-worth. Lederach (2003:48-60) suggests that a transformative approach to conflict in schools will require teachers and other staff to develop capacities in:

- seeing incidents as windows onto underlying issues, so not seeking quick fixes and short-term solutions

- being simultaneously short-term responsive and long-term strategic, so dealing with multiple time-frames

- posing problems as dilemmas, and therefore to engage in both/and thinking rather than either/or – both long-term and short-term, both the big picture and the specific detail – and to live with complexities and paradoxes

- seeing complexity as a friend not a foe, so being trusting not rigid

- hearing and engaging with 'the voices of identity' (Lederach, 2003: 55), and encouraging people to articulate a positive sense of their own identity in relationships with others, but not to fear, blame or demean them.

The development of such capacities, Lederach points out, often involves music, the arts, rituals, dialogue-as-sport, fun and laughter. Essentially, it requires a climate characterised by both security and challenge.

Climate

Unlike most other aspects of education, training events in the field of race equality involve political controversy – there is a wide range of views amongst participants, and an even wider and more obvious range in society at large. In certain sections of the media there is much negative coverage of certain communities in modern society, particularly Muslims, people seeking asylum, migrants from eastern Europe, African-Caribbeans and Gypsies and Travellers. Also there is negative coverage, as discussed in chapter 1, of so-called political correctness and of multiculturalism. This pervasive context of controversy creates stress or potential stress for teachers.

As well as being controversial, the topic of race equality is sensitive. Teachers have to come to terms with their own feelings and biases – including guilt, shame, resentment and anger – and may be challenged to change deeply-held views of themselves, of national story and history ('I too am America'), and of wider society. Further, they may have to re-think their understanding of the nature and responsibilities of professionalism.

It follows that training events in this field need to have certain distinctive characteristics. A successful training course in the field of race equality, it is argued here, has a climate with six components. These are like separate stages or phases in the sense that they belong to a sequence, and that the quality of the last depends on the components that have come earlier. However, the metaphor of strand, as distinct from the metaphor of stage, is valuable and relevant also. The six components are of equal importance. An alternative metaphor can be drawn from music. There are six motifs. All are latent throughout and for all there are prefigurings and reprises but each has its own time to be dominant. The six components of an effective climate are:

- feeling secure, known, trusted and respected
- feeling challenged
- examining case-studies and stories
- encountering theories
- formulating principles to guide further action
- making specific plans.

At the risk of over-simplification, these six components can be memorised with the initial letters of the word A-G-E-N-D-A:

- A: *being accepted, acknowledged and affirmed,* and in consequence feeling secure, trusted and respected

- G: *getting to grips with grievances,* and in this way being challenged

- E: *encountering and examining endeavours and exploits,* by attending to case-studies, stories and narratives

- N: *noting notions and nuances,* by engaging with theoretical writings and talks

- D: *discussing, debating, deliberating and declaring,* by drawing up statements of principles to guide further action

- A: *agreeing actions to be undertaken,* by making specific plans.

Professional development is cyclical rather than linear. This point is nicely expressed by the word AGENDA, for the first and last letters are the same. The action with which one cycle of learning finishes is also the action which is affirmed at the start of a new cycle. Learning is a continuous revolution.

The first two components of an effective climate are security and challenge. A prerequisite for developing these is an appeal to a range of learning styles. The same appeal will provide security for some participants but challenge for others, for participants will vary in relation to matters such as:

- tolerance of ambiguity and uncertainty, or else desire for clarity and precision

- preparedness or otherwise to admit ignorance and to make mistakes

- whether they prefer to learn about the whole – 'the big picture' – before the parts, or the parts before the whole

- how much they like visual material, or else prefer text

- how much they like to be active, using their hands and moving around, or be passively listening and absorbing

- the extent to which they like their emotions and personalities as well as their intellect to be involved

- the extent to which they like to consider the human and political implications of the topic under consideration

- the extent to which they are inclined to question and challenge what they are told, and the person who is telling them

- whether they enjoy working with symbols and metaphors, or prefer to take things literally

- the extent to which they need to talk before they can understand something, or to talk even before they know what their ideas are – 'I don't know what I think till I hear what I say'.

These differences need to be acknowledged and catered for. The fact remains that how educators teach is what they teach – the message is in the methodology they use as well as in the content they present. It is paradoxical and self-defeating to run a training course in which key concepts are equality, dignity, empowerment, deliberative democracy and mutual respect, without incorporating these values in the methodology, rather than just lecturing about them. It follows there must be much use of small group work. In the early stages of a course this arguably needs to be tightly focused by activities and exercises that may risk being over-structured but too little structure at the start of a course is a greater danger than too much.

Two introductory activities are described below. The first involves each individual jotting notes as a private aide-memoire. Other things being equal it is easier to talk with others, and to be attentive to others, if one has first tidied and sorted out one's own mind. Participants are given a proforma and asked to respond to these four triggers:

The sights and sounds of home
Images and happenings in my mind's eye from the first six or so years of my life

Grandparents
Stories, sayings, advice, warnings, comment from my grandparents and their generation

Journeys
Treks, visits, travels, holidays, moves I have made over the years

Home again
Memories of re-entries and returns when I came back home

Participants then introduce themselves, using the private notes they have jotted, in groups of four or six. It is reasonable to expect an activity such as this will lead to each individual feeling secure, known, trusted and respected, a somebody at the course, not a nobody. And it is reasonable too to expect that people will find each other interesting and stimulating, and well worth getting to know better, in order to learn from interaction with them. Further, to recall the metaphor in this chapter's title, they are beginning to establish the dining-table of shared responsibility. A possible title for the proforma is 'Homes and Journeys'. People are subliminally reminded that the interflow between the security of home and the adventure of going forth is a continual oscillation throughout life.

Course participants, they are reminded, are taking part in this interflow at this very moment. They have left their homes and workplaces earlier in the day and soon will be returning. In the meanwhile, the group of people whom they are getting to know round the table at this training event are to be their base or home during the course itself. They will be leaving it to encounter and work with other course members but will be returning to it to report back and reflect.

At any training event there are likely to be anxieties about so-called political correctness. Sometimes people may feel they dare not open their mouths for fear of using the 'wrong' word and being seen and perhaps labelled by others as behind the times or racist. Such anxieties need to be acknowledged, not swept under the carpet (Sardar, 2008). Otherwise they may remain an elephant in the room, and prevent or impede learning. One simple and straightforward way of respecting anxieties around appropriate language, and of making them manageable, is to provide various pairs or groups of words. Participants work in pairs or threes to discuss the nuances and implications of different words and to agree, if they can, on the meanings of words they will accept as common currency and those they will not use. Contested words include:

- equality/diversity
- cohesion/integration/inclusion
- race/ethnicity

- Great Britain/United Kingdom
- religion/faith/spirituality/belief
- Islamophobia/anti-Muslim racism
- Islamic/Islamist
- racism/xenophobia
- prejudice/discrimination
- narrative/story/history/myth
- Derry/Londonderry
- orthodox/conservative/fundamentalist/traditional
- extremist/radical/fanatical/zealous
- BME people/ethnic minority people/people of colour
- asylum seekers/people seeking asylum

The discussions of words such as these are necessarily discussions about the nature of language. It is these latter discussions which are of great value. Participants are reminded that words change in their meanings and implications over time, and mean different things to different people. This is a fact of life, and not something to be terribly bothered about. Changes of language occur partly because the outer world changes; partly because understandings of the world change; and partly because various groups and communities ('speech communities') gain greater power and influence than hitherto, and therefore more access to platforms and committee tables, and can make their voices, understandings and definitions better known. So anxieties and uncertainties about linguistic change are often bound up with anxieties about changing relationships and changing patterns of influence and power. As mentioned in chapter 1, concerns in the media about so-called political correctness are arguably connected with concerns about social change both nationally and globally, not just about language.

Different words are used in different contexts. With regard to discourse about 'race' in the UK, for example, there tend to be differences between usage in four different forums: a) official documents b) most ordinary conversation amongst white people, reflected and reinforced in the media c) usage reflecting the self-understanding of individuals and communities at the receiving end of prejudice and discrimination, and d) usage in academia.

The choice of a word frequently indicates the speech community to which a person belongs or with which they wish to identify. For example, Derry and Londonderry in Northern Ireland are the same place but a different name is used by different communities. If you ask a stranger how to get there you indicate not only literally where you want to go but also, metaphorically, where you are coming from. 'The limits of my language,' said Wittgenstein, 'are the limits of my world'.

After introductory activities in home groups such as those described above, it is often appropriate to organise a so-called jigsaw exercise. This involves people negotiating and agreeing with other members of their home group about what each will do within a simple option scheme. They leave home in order to take part in the scheme and in due course they return to their base group and report back. The activity of reporting back is invaluable for helping people to internalise what they have learned; further, it communicates a sense of trust in participants' capacity to act as teachers for each other. The options may include:

- sorting and discussing a range of scenarios and critical incidents in schools, for example those which are listed in table 4.1 in chapter 4; the task with each story is to consider what should happen in the next few minutes, the next few days and the next few weeks, and in this way to clarify the underlying issues

- sorting, discussing and ranking a set of quotations from the media of the last fortnight or so; amongst other things, this gives a vivid sense of topicality, and is a reminder of racism, bigotry and ignorance in sections of the media and in the general climate of public opinion

- sequencing a set of quotations from various documents, speeches and interviews over the last 100 years, all of them about an aspect of racism; this gives a sense of change and continuity over time and enables difficult and sensitive material to be – if each quotation is provided on a separate slip of paper – literally manageable

- sequencing sentences cut from a piece of theoretical writing, for example the piece of writing about race and racism in chapter 3 of this book

- writing messages and replies to real enquiries and requests for advice and assistance on the helpline of the *Times Educational Supplement*

- browsing through a collection of textbooks and packs, and writing brief evaluative reviews of some of them

- surfing the Internet to find nuggets and snippets to incorporate into a personal scrapbook or blog.

The activities listed above all contain elements of E and N – enquiries and notions – in the A-G-E-N-D-A mnemonic, for they involve encounters with case studies, stories and practical projects and initiatives, and discussing and evaluating a range of theoretical perspectives. The last two elements, D and A, are deliberating and agreeing on action. As a preliminary to making practical plans for projects they themselves will embark on, participants may consider key ideas across the curriculum, as outlined in chapter 6. All too often, discussions of a multicultural curriculum are still limited to being little more than about the infamous 3 S's of the 1970s – saris, samosas and steel bands. Consideration of key ideas confronts such simplistic approaches but also places teaching about cultures in an appropriate context. Participants can be given summaries of the six major ideas in chapter 6 on separate pieces of paper or card and set the task of working in small groups to put them into a logical sequence. Further, as a way of fixing the ideas in their consciousness and memory, they may select a postcard with which to illustrate each idea.

Finally, participants formulate plans for things they themselves will do in their own workplaces. The plans should include, although certainly not be limited to, consideration of constraints and possible problems and how these will be dealt with. It is valuable if participants act as professional friends and consultants for each other. The task is to ask supportive and facilitating questions rather than to give outright advice. Ideally, participants meet again in due course and report on what they have done. The agenda then starts again, with the action planned at the end of the first cycle being that which is affirmed at the start of the next.

Concluding note

'Something to bring back, to show you have been there.' The words are down-to-earth, ordinary, prosaic. They could be a statement of what someone hopes to gain when they go to an inservice session or course as part of their continuing professional development. In point of fact, though, they are the opening two lines of a poem by R S Thomas. The typical things someone might bring back to their workplace, according to Thomas, are not handouts or copies of powerpoint slides but, he says, 'a lock of God's hair stolen from him while he was asleep' and 'a photograph of the garden of the spirit'. He goes on to remind himself and his readers that the point of going somewhere is 'not to arrive but to return home'. And one returns home, he adds, 'laden with pollen you shall work up into the honey the mind feeds on'. Well, not a bad summary, allowing for poetic licence, of what might one hope to gain from a training session!

The metaphors recall that learning is mysterious and transformative, and its outcomes cannot be wholly predicted or determined in advance. The general process, however, can most certainly be described. It's a process that should 'force us to contemplate our humanity, it's got to make us think about love and care and concern and kindness ... We've got to come to a position collectively, where we agree that guilt and blame have no place at the dining table of shared responsibility.'

CONCLUSION

12

What works and what does not work
Drawing themes and threads together

During the focus groups and workshops which are the basis of chapter 2, young people were asked to make suggestions about immediate steps their schools might take to put an end to racist bullying. Their answers touched on many of the themes and threads of this book. First, there was recurring emphasis on the need to listen to the stories, voices and experiences of people such as themselves. This book started with the experience of a boy at a school in Greater Manchester and continued in chapter 2 with many quotations from young people. It is essential that teachers and other staff should know what's going on in their pupils' lives. The pupils came up with thoughtful ideas.

> Consult pupils about what works and what does not work.

> All staff must listen to pupils if they are telling them about racist bullying.

> Ask children what bullying is going on.

Such consultation can take a variety of forms, and structures need to be maintained which give pupils opportunities to explain and describe, such as:

> Have a named teacher who understands and who pupils can trust for them to go to.

> Have a place in school where people can come for help.

> Have more of a presence at break and lunch times and have more of a watchful eye.

> Have an anonymous box so people can put notes in it about what racist things have happened to them or others, or make suggestions.

Have agony aunts. This can be by email. It could also be someone you could go to or write to by suggestion box.

Have pupils who can help. It could be playground buddies with special hats and badges so everyone knows them. Then if someone is getting problems you can go to them and they will play with you. It could be special representatives on the school council. You can tell them what is happening and they will pass it on.

Have helpline numbers available on posters around the school, or on cards pupils can carry.

Second, there were references to the qualities and capacities required of staff. Some of these are to do with intellectual understanding, for example of racism and bullying, as discussed in chapter 3, of different ways of dealing with incidents (chapter 4), and of handling controversial and sensitive issues (chapters 7 and 10). Others are more to do with values, emotions and personal commitments – hearts as well as minds (chapters 9 and 11). Suggestions and recommendations included:

Teachers and school staff should have extra training, including supply teachers.

Acknowledge that racism and bullying exist.

Let pupils know where you stand.

Have more PSHE and RE lessons and more Circle Time and discuss racism and bullying.

A third point, implicit in many of the quotations above and explicit frequently through this book, is that everyone has a part to play.

Make sure everyone in school is involved and knows what they can do.

Tell parents what's been going on about this.

To echo the title of the previous chapter there needs to be shared responsibility. The immediate reference in chapter 11 was to Asian, black and white people working together, beyond recriminations and guilt. More broadly, this book is about shared responsibility in many other contexts as well: teachers, administrative staff and support staff in schools; staff in schools, school governors, parents and local communities; services for children and young people and the police service; and, most centrally and importantly of all, both adults and the young.

The long-term goal, it was suggested in chapter 4, can be described as nothing less than transformation: the transformation of schools and society, and also of individual human beings – a project 'changed me completely into a new kind of person,' said a young person quoted at the start of chapter 9 about a piece of theatre. Another thread running though this book is the role of the arts – not only theatre but also fiction, poetry, music and sport. The arts and sport provide both security and challenge and have a key role in helping to transform bystanders into active citizens.

It is fitting that the last words in this book should be provided by children and young people. Here, repeated from chapter 2, are some of their voices:

> We want a school where all pupils can be proud of themselves and their cultures, and of each other.

> Racism is wrong and it affects a lot of people.

> Schools should make sure everyone in school knows what they can do. Make sure that parents, teachers, caretakers, learning support assistants, cleaning staff – everybody – is involved. Tell the parents to talk.

> Tell everyone – Never join in with bullying or fights. Join together to say NO.

> I have the right to be treated the same as everyone else: nicely, kindly, fairly.

> I have the right for no-one to be unkind to me because of my colour or religion. I have the right to work in a safe place, where there is no bullying. I have the right to be listened to.

ACKNOWLEDGEMENTS

Some of the material in this book arises from the authors' involvement in the production of *Preventing and Addressing Racism in Schools*, published by Ealing Education Department in 2003, and *Bullying around Racism, Culture and Religion: how to prevent it and what to do when it happens*, web-published by the Department for Education and Skills in 2006. Chapters 7 and 11 draw in part on articles which first appeared in the journal *Race Equality Teaching*. Chapter 8 draws on work undertaken for Kick It Out.

Production of the DfES publication was led and co-ordinated at the DfES by Teresa Clark and her colleagues Charlotte Sowerbutts, Eric Oyewole and Sarah Willett, and involved substantial consultation with local authorities and individuals. In this latter connection it drew on work in Brighton and Hove, Buckinghamshire, Cambridgeshire, Coventry, Cumbria, Dorset, Derbyshire, Ealing, East Sussex, Greenwich, Hampshire, Lancashire, Leeds, Leicester, Manchester, Oldham, Staffordshire, Wiltshire, Windsor and Maidenhead, and Wolverhampton.

Individuals who contributed to the DfES project included headteachers and teachers, local authority officers, advisers and inspectors, members of community and voluntary organisations, children and young people, academics and civil servants. The participants in a 24-hour writing workshop were Teresa Clark, Gill Francis, Chris Gaine, Richard Gore, John Khan, Jane Lane, Berenice Miles, Paulette North, Robin Richardson, Shaila Shaikh, Charlotte Sowerbutts, Yvette Thomas and Sarah Willett. The speakers and principal contributors at consultative conferences included most of those mentioned above and also Rita Adair, Peter Barton, Maud Blair, Babette Brown, Margaret Cadman, Pamela Carroll, Maurice Coles, Emma Jane Cross, Adrienne Katz, Kate Hinton, Carol Hunte, Ruth Kerry, Arthur Ivatts, Kevin Love, Ian Massey, Rehana Minhas, Peter Nathan, John O'Brien, Ray Priest, Mandeep Rupra, Jill Rutter, Tim Spafford, John Stead, Eilidh Verhoeven, Anne Walker and Linda Walker.

The authors owe a great debt of gratitude to those with whom they have worked over the years, including especially those mentioned above, and to the projects in which they have been involved. Views expressed or implied in this book, however, are their responsibility alone and do not necessarily reflect the views of any of the individuals or institutions mentioned above.

APPENDICES

Appendix A
Questions for school evaluation

Introductory note

Schools are required to evaluate the extent to which pupils feel safe and adopt safe practices. As part of this they are prompted to consider whether learners feel safe from bullying and racist incidents, and the extent to which pupils feel confident to talk to staff and others when they feel at risk. Inspectors will routinely seek views from pupils about their experience, including whether they feel free from bullying and harassment.

This paper lists questions which schools may wish to ask themselves. It is derived from Ofsted's thematic report *Race Equality in Education* (November 2005) and from conferences, consultations and meetings which took place in 2005-06 in connection with DfES web-based guidance, *Bullying around Race, Culture and Religion – how to prevent it and what to do when it happens* (www.teachernet.gov.uk/racistbullying).

Not all the points in this list are equally urgent and relevant in all schools. They are offered as a menu from which to select, not tick-list or score-sheet whose every item should be considered in turn. Schools may find the evaluation useful when preparing their race equality policy, and robust evidence for the SEF.

Documentation

1. Has documentation about dealing with racist incidents been thoroughly discussed by, and is it kept under review by, pupils and parents as well as by staff?

2. Do we have a written code of practice which clearly outlines specific procedures to be followed for recording and dealing with racist bullying, as also with other kinds of abuse and bullying, on the school premises, and on journeys to and from school?

3. Is our commitment to preventing and addressing racism and bullying clearly stated in posters and displays in corridors and classrooms?

Discussion, monitoring and review

4. Is there shared understanding amongst staff – including support and administrative staff as well as teachers – of ways in which bullying based on background, colour, religion or heritage is both similar to and different from other kinds of bullying?

5. Do we train lunchtime staff and learning mentors to identify racist bullying and to follow school policy and procedures on anti-bullying?

6. Does a senior member of staff have responsibility for ensuring that incidents of racist bullying are appropriately dealt with and recorded?

The perceptions and involvement of children and young people

7. Do we take practical steps to ensure we are aware of pupils' experiences, for example through anonymous surveys and reporting, and through focus group discussions?

8. Do pupils consider that the school has a history of taking racist incidents seriously and following them up?

9. Has a user-friendly leaflet been provided for pupils and their parents on what to do if they experience racism against them?

10. Ofsted states that responses to racist bullying should be 'swift, proportionate, discreet, influential and effective'. Do pupils agree that this is how their own school operates?

11. Are pupils involved in mediating in disputes and in peer mentoring?

Ethos and curriculum

12. Do we give a high profile to rights and responsibilities by, for example, promoting the United Nations Convention on the Rights of the Child and the UNICEF programme on Rights Respecting Schools?

13. Does the general ethos of the school (displays, assemblies, some of the examples across the curriculum) reflect and affirm diversity of language, culture, religion and appearance?

14. Many analyses state that bullying can be a result of feeling powerless. What is our school doing to ensure that none of our children and young people feel powerless in the school community?

15 Do we include the histories, contributions and achievements of a range of societies in our teaching content? Do we ensure that their perspectives and viewpoints are reflected in the way we teach?'

16. Is the school involved from time to time in national projects such as *Kick Racism Out Of Football*, *Islamic Awareness Week*, *One World Week*, *Black History Month*, *Anti-Bullying Week* and *Refugee Week*?

17. Have we reviewed opportunities in the national curriculum to teach about various kinds of intolerance and prejudice, and the values of justice, fairness and non-discrimination?

18. Do we make good use of drama, role-play, creative writing, music and art in our teaching about bullying and behaviour?

19. Do we have an agreed statement and policy on teaching and talking about emotive and controversial issues?

20. Do we use the strategies developed by projects such as Philosophy for Children (P4C)?

Working with parents

21. Do parents know who to contact if they are worried about bullying?

22. Do we work with parents and other people in the local community to address tensions beyond the school gates that may be played out within school?

23. Do we make our commitments on countering racist bullying clear at parents' induction meetings?

24. Are parents confident that the school deals effectively and sensitively with incidents of racist bullying?

Partnership working

25. Do we have good working relationships with the police and with voluntary sector organisations and networks concerned with racial harassment issues?

26. Do we make good use of guidance and advice provided by the local authority in connection with preventing and addressing bullying around racism, culture and religion?

Development: prejudice-based bullying more generally

27. Have we considered, or may we consider, developing policy and procedures on other forms of prejudice-based bullying? For example, bullying around sexual harassment and homophobia, and disabilities and special needs?

Appendix B
The legal framework in England

Legislation and government guidance	Duties of schools in relation to preventing and addressing racist bullying
Every Child Matters	Every Child Matters is legislation for the well-being of children and young people from birth to age 19. The issues of racism, bullying and children participating in decision-making are included in three of the five priorities: being healthy, staying safe and enjoying and achieving. Examples of items schools have to report on are: **4b To what extent do learners feel safe and adopt safe practices?** ■ whether learners feel safe from bullying and racist incidents ■ the extent to which learners have confidence to talk to staff and others when they feel at risk. **4d How well do learners make a positive contribution to the community?** ■ learners' growing understanding of their rights and responsibilities, and of those of others ■ how well learners express their views and contribute to communal activities. **Judgement on leadership and management** How well equality of opportunity is promoted and discrimination tackled so that all learners achieve as well as they can.
National Curriculum	The national curriculum for England and Wales was revised to take effect from September 2008, and targets specifically intended to combat racism were introduced, notably teaching about the transatlantic slave trade. The citizenship and PSHE curriculum areas have targets for teaching about racism and bullying.

Legislation and government guidance	Duties of schools in relation to preventing and addressing racist bullying
Ofsted inspections	Under the new arrangements for Ofsted inspections schools complete a self-evaluation form (SEF) which the inspectors discuss with the school. Ofsted says: *The self evaluation form (SEF) is at the heart of the new inspection arrangements – it serves as the main document when planning the inspection with the school, and is crucial in evaluating the quality of leadership and management and the school's capacity to improve.* **http://www.ofsted.gov.uk/schools/sef.cfm** Throughout the SEF reference is made to promoting equality and combating racism and bullying. It appears in sections on achievement (3), personal development and well-being (4), making a positive contribution to the community and community cohesion (4), and curriculum (5). Section 6, leadership and management, strongly reinforces the management role in all of these issues.
The Race Relations (Amendment) Act	The Race Relations Amendment Act places three general duties on all public bodies, including schools: ■ to eliminate discrimination ■ to promote equality of opportunity ■ to promote good race relations All state schools must : ■ actively promote race equality ■ prepare a race equality policy ■ monitor attainment by ethnicity, using new electronic data systems ■ monitor exclusions by ethnicity ■ monitor progress and make the information publicly accessible
Recording and reporting racist incidents	Schools are required to record all racist incidents, take action to address them, and to report to the local authority on the number of incidents and the numbers they have followed up. Until March 2008 local authorities were required to report aggregated information to the Audit Commission as part of the local authority best value performance indicators: BVPI 174 and 175. New arrangements from April 2008 to cut down the number of local authority performance indicators to 198 mean authorities are continuing to collect the information to monitor

Legislation and government guidance	Duties of schools in relation to preventing and addressing racist bullying
	that the government no longer collects these statistics except in the case of race hate crime. Early indications are that local authorities are continuing to collect the information to monitor the trends in their areas. Guidance from Ofsted expects schools to collect the information as part of good practice in meeting their duties under the Race Relations Act. The Stephen Lawrence inquiry definition of a racist incident is used: *A racist incident is any incident which is perceived to be racist by the victim or any other person.* The school's procedures for addressing racism and bullying make good evidence for section 4 of the Ofsted school self-evaluation form (see above).
Community cohesion	Under the Education and Inspections Act (EIA) 2006, from 1 September 2007 the governing bodies of maintained schools have the duty to promote community cohesion. Government papers related to the new duty make it clear that it relates to and complements the duties in the Race Relations Amendment Act 2000. The Department for Children, Schools and Families (DCSF) issued guidance on the duty in July 2007. The full guidance can be downloaded from the Teachernet website. The guidance defines three broad areas under which the school's contribution to community cohesion can be grouped: ■ teaching, learning and curriculum ■ equity and excellence ■ engagement and extended services. Ofsted inspections of the contribution that schools make to community cohesion started in September 2008. The government's community cohesion education standards for schools define a cohesive community as one where: ■ there is a common vision and a sense of belonging for all communities ■ the diversity of people's different backgrounds and circumstances is appreciated and positively valued ■ those from different backgrounds have similar life opportunities ■ strong and positive relationships are being developed between people from different

Legislation and government guidance	Duties of schools in relation to preventing and addressing racist bullying
	backgrounds in the workplace, in schools and within neighbourhoods.
	The four strategic aims of the Community Cohesion Standards are to: ■ close the attainment and achievement gap ■ develop common values of citizenship based on dialogue, mutual respect and acceptance of diversity ■ contribute to building good community relations and challenge all types of discrimination and inequality ■ remove the barriers to access, participation, progression, attainment and achievement. The Community Cohesion Education Standard for Schools provides a clear and helpful breakdown of what each of these strategic aims means for schools, and what schools should do to ensure they are met. This advice is set out in the introduction to the standard, on the School Standards website. The community cohesion curriculum has been influenced by the Ajegbo report, and is intended to be a tool for countering racism in all its forms.
School attendance	Schools are required to report all unauthorised absences to the DCSF. Research shows that a high proportion of pupils who are bullied keep away from school, and there is a correlation between poor attendance and poor achievement.

Appendix C
Useful websites

Anne Frank House
Websites about teaching about antisemitism and racism through the inspiration of Anne Frank's diary are accessible through the site of Anne Frank House, based in Amsterdam. **www.annefrank.org**

Anti-Defamation League
Lesson plans and resource lists for teaching about a wide range of equality and diversity issues under the general heading of anti-bias teaching. Based in the United States, but with stimulating ideas for many other countries as well. **http://www.adl.org/education/**

Antiracist Toolkit
Advice on good practice on a range of matters, including dealing with racist behaviour in schools and developing a positive school ethos. Many case studies. Developed in Scotland but relevant throughout the UK, and indeed in many other countries. **www.antiracisttoolkit.org.uk**

Antisectarian Education
'Don't give it, don't take it': definitions and vivid practical suggestions for primary and secondary classrooms, with a section on Islamophobia. Intended for schools across Scotland, but the approaches are relevant in many other contexts.
http://www.ltscotland.org.uk/antisectarian/index.asp

Atlantic Slave Trade and life in the Americas
Copyright-free images and maps from history.
http://hitchcock.itc.virginia.edu/Slavery/search.html

BBC Newsround
Useful and stimulating lesson plans and materials for teaching about racism and leading discussion of, and action against, racist bullying.
http://news.bbc.co.uk/cbbcnews/hi/newsid_4020000/newsid_4025100/4025117.stm

Black Information Link

Run by the 1990 Trust, a large collection of newspaper articles, cuttings and reports, all clearly catalogued, giving a comprehensive picture of the current scene.
www.blink.org.uk

Bradford Antiracist Projects

Papers about race equality issues in schools and news of events and publications.
www.barp.org.uk

Breaking the Silence

Powerful, interactive material for researching the transatlantic slave trade and current issues of slavery and oppression.
http://www.antislavery.org/breakingthesilence/index.shtml

Britkid

Intended in the first instance for primary school pupils in areas where there are few people of minority backgrounds, but its application is much wider.
www.britkid.org/

Brycchan Carey

Bycchan Carey is a senior lecturer in English literature who has written extensively on the transatlantic slave trade. His website is clear and packed with information.
http://www.brycchancarey.com/index.htm

Caribbean Guide

Good website for the history of the Caribbean, including information on slave rebellions.
http://caribbean-guide.info/past.and.present/history/abolition/index.html

Center for Holocaust and Genocide Studies

Based at the University of Minnesota, many resources for teachers, including poetry and a series of articles on 'visualising otherness'.
http://www.chgs.umn.edu/

Channel 4 Race Debate

Broadcasters, actors, musicians and writers share their experiences and describe the reality of multiculturalism in Britain today. There is also an 'ethnicity map of Britain', with a wealth of useful facts and statistics.
http://www.channel4.com/culture/microsites/R/racedebate/talkingpoint/

Coastkid

Based on the Britkid concept (see above) and based in Brighton and Hove, the focus is on the relationships and conflicts that arise between nine young people in an imaginary school. **http://www.coastkid.org/**

Commission on British Muslims and Islamophobia

The full text of the Commission's 2004 report, plus also some extracts from it, including *Islamophobia and Race Relations and Debate and Disagreement*.
www.insted.co.uk/islam.html

Cross-community forum

Projects on the transatlantic slave trade and current issues of slavery and oppression.
http://www.antislavery.org/archive/press/pressrelease2005bicentenary.htm

Crosspoint

Descriptions of, and links to numerous antiracist organisations and projects, including many with a local focus. The link takes you to the UK section but elsewhere on the site there is information from over 100 other countries.
http://www.magenta.nl/crosspoint/uk.html

Facing History

'By studying the historical development and the legacies of the Holocaust and other instances of collective violence students learn to combat prejudice with compassion ... myth and misinformation with knowledge.' Invaluable for teaching about antisemitism and also other forms of racism, and about current and recent issues.
www.FacingHistory.com

Ekta Kettering

Run for teenagers by teenagers, about racist attacks and attitudes. Based in a single borough but with relevance and interest everywhere. **http://www.ektakettering.org/**

Football Unites

Campaigns against racism in and around football grounds are a significant development in recent years. Much valuable information from the Football Unites Racism Divides project, set up by Sheffield United. **www.furd.org**

Forum Against Islamophobia and Racism

Useful range of recent newspaper articles and several valuable factsheets. Valuable newsletter several times a week. **http://www.fairuk.org/**

Freedom

Excellent teaching resource from various museums in Britain.
http://www.nmm.ac.uk/freedom/

Freedom Fighters

Substantial information about resistance, rebellion and emancipation.
http://www.geocities.com/CollegePark/Classroom/9912/freedomfighters.html

Guardian Newspaper

Special section archiving all articles and reports about race equality since 1998. Also, there are links to other relevant sections, for example on British Islam and Multicultural London. **www.guardian.co.uk/race**

Hometown

Set up by the Anti-Bullying Alliance (ABA), this is a lively and engaging site for children about dealing with bullying, including racist bullying. Lots of conversations and stories for role-play, discussion and further research.
http://www.anti-bullyingalliance.org/walkthru.htm

Human Rights and Equal Opportunity Commission

The official government site in Australia dealing with anti-discrimination legislation. Section on race includes some excellent teaching materials on media treatment of refugees and immigration that are readily transferable to UK contexts. The link takes you straight to them.
http://www.hreoc.gov.au/info_for_teachers/face_facts03/index.htm

Institute of Race Relations

Many key articles and a large archive of links to news items in the local press throughout UK, and a valuable weekly newsletter about current events. **www.irr.org.uk**

Jamaicaway

Website dedicated to information on the national heroes of Jamaica. It includes Nanny, Paul Bogle and Sam Sharpe.
http://www.jamaicaway.com/Heroes/index.html#heroindex

Kick It Out

The national campaign against racism in football. The website includes useful materials for schools, as does that of *Show Racism the Red Card* (see below).
http://www.kickitout.org/

Kiddiesville Football Club

Intended particularly for primary schools, a lively site about the exploits of an imaginary football team, with music, stories, games, humorous and nonsense verse, and vivid graphics. Also, explanatory background notes for teachers ('Adultsville'.) Highly recommended. **www.kiddiesvillefc.com**

Lift Off Project

Lively and imaginative materials and activities for human rights education.
http://www.amnesty.org.uk/content.asp?CategoryID=748

Monitoring Group
A large archive of news items about racist attacks throughout Britain, and about actions and campaigns to prevent them. **http://www.monitoring-group.co.uk/**

National Assembly Against Racism
Large archive of news stories and topical commentary, updated several times a month. **http://www.naar.org.uk/**

Persona Dolls
The Dolls and their stories are powerful tools for exploring and confronting bias. **www.persona-doll-training.org**

Positive Images
Wide range of posters presenting aspects of positive images and black history. **http://www.multicultural-art.co.uk/black.html**

Qualifications and Curriculum Authority: bigotry and prejudice
Lesson plans on teaching about antisemitism using *The Diary of Anne Frank* (KS2), challenging racism through circle time (KS1), refugees and human rights (KS3) and racial discrimination (KS4). **www.qca.org.uk/ca.inclusion/respect_for_all.**

Racism No Way
Fact sheets, classroom activities, quizzes, webquests, news items and links to recent articles from around the world. **http://www.racismnoway.com.au/**

Rewind
A lively collection of materials and discussions about racism and race equality for secondary students, teachers and youth workers. **www.rewind.org.uk**

Sectarianism – don't give it, don't take it
Lively resources, guidance and ideas for teachers in Scotland, widely relevant. **http://www.ltscotland.org.uk/antisectarian/**

Set All Free
Website produced by Churches Together in England, with comprehensive resources for the bicentenary in 2007. Although it is primarily for Christian churches, much is useful for teachers in mainstream schools. **http://www.setallfree.net/**

Show Racism the Red Card
The national campaign against racism in football, with much material of direct interest to pupils. There is also a site on the same theme in Scotland. **www.srtrc.org** **http://www.theredcardscotland.org/**

Spartacus Schoolnet

Clear and extremely comprehensive website for school use, with biographies of the major participants in abolition, including lists of women who participated, anti-slavery societies, plantation life, historical events and more.
http://www.spartacus.schoolnet.co.uk/slavery.htm

Understanding Slavery

Many valuable resources and links to other sites.
http://www.understandingslavery.com/

UNESCO

International historical material about the abolition of the slave trade, including bio-graphies.**http://portal.unesco.org/culture/en/ev.php-URL_ID=5420&URL_DO=DO_ TOPIC& URL_SECTION=201.html**

Untold London

Information, timelines and stories about London's communities.
http://www.untoldlondon.org.uk/collections/AM16435.html

Bibliography

Ajegbo, Keith, chair of committee (2006) Diversity and Citizenship Curriculum Review, London: Department for Education and Skills

Alexander, Jenny (2003) *Bullies, Bigmouths and So-called Friends*, London: Hodder Children's Books

Appiah, Kwame Anthony (2006) *Cosmopolitanism: ethics in a world of strangers*, London: Allen Lane

Association for Media Literacy (n.d.) What is media literacy?, web-published at http://www.aml.ca/whatis/ (last accessed July 2008)

Association of Psychological Science (2008) Sticks and Stones: a new study on social and physical pain, *Psychological Science*, press release, August 2008

Baig, Anila (2007) 'Multiculturalism in Britain today: has it worked?', Channel Four, http://www.channel4.com/culture/microsites/R/racedebate/talkingpoint/feature/anila-baig.html (accessed July 2008)

Ball, Sue (2006) *Bystanders and Bullying: a summary of research for anti-bullying week,* London: Anti-Bullying Alliance

Banks, James A. *et al* (2005) *Democracy and Diversity: principles and concepts for educating citizens in a global age*, Seattle WA: Center for Multicultural Education, University of Washington

Barton, Peter and Norman Schamroth (2004) Understanding Differences, Valuing Diversity: tackling racism through story, drama and video in mainly white primary schools, *Race Equality Teaching* vol 23 no 1, autumn

Bednall, Jane and Nirvana Culora, Sharon Fell, Jane Handscomb, Maggie Hewitt (2007) *Developing a Culturally Inclusive Curriculum*, London: Newham and Mantra Lingua

Besag, Val (2007) *Understanding Girls' Friendships, Fights and Feuds – a practical approach to girls' bullying*, Maidenhead: Open University Press

Boal, Augusto (1992) *Games for Actors and Non-Actors*, London: Routledge

Braverman, Danny (2002) *Playing a Part: drama and citizenship*, Stoke on Trent: Trentham Books

Britten, Nick (2006) 'CPS 'is crazy' to take playtime insults to court', *The Daily Telegraph*, 7 April

British Psychological Society (2006) *Submission to Education and Skills Select Committee Inquiry into Bullying,* London: British Psychological Society

Brown, Babette (2008) *Equality in Action: a way forward with Persona Dolls*, Stoke on Trent: Trentham Books

Brown, Rupert and Adam Rutland, Charles Watters (2008) *Identities in Transition: a longitudinal study of immigrant children*, ESRC press release 24 July 2008, London: Economic and Social Research Council

Bunyan, Nigel (2006) 'Lawyers drop case of schoolboy with racist taunts', *Daily Telegraph*, 27 April

Campbell, Charlie (2008) 'Racist incidents in schools at new high', *Redbridge Guardian and West Essex Gazette*, 1 April

Carroll, Pamela (2004) Festival of Fools: tackling racism in schools without a script, *Race Equality Teaching*, vol 22 no 2, spring

Citizenship Foundation (2003) *Education for Citizenship, Diversity and Race Equality: a practical guide,* London: Citizenship Foundation and Me Too

Claire, Hilary and Cathie Holden eds (2007) *The Challenge of Teaching Controversial Issues*, Stoke on Trent: Trentham Books

Cline, Tony with Guida de Abreu, Cornelius Fihosy, Hilary Gray, Hannah Lambert and Jo Neale (2002) *Minority Ethnic Pupils in Mainly White Schools: research report RR 365,* Department for Education and Skills

Coles, Maurice Irfan (2008) *Every Muslim Child Matters: practical guidance for schools and children's services*, Stoke on Trent: Trentham Books

Coloroso, Barbara (2005) *The Bully, The Bullied and The Bystander: from preschool to secondary school – how parents and teachers can help break the cycle of violence*, London: Piccadilly Press

Commission on the Future of Multi-Ethnic Britain (2000) *The Future of Multi-Ethnic Britain: the Parekh report*, London: Profile Books for the Runnymede Trust

Commission on Integration and Cohesion (2007) *Our Shared Future*, Department for Communities and Local Government

Cumbria Education Service (2004) *Ally Comes to Cumbria: teaching resource to support antiracist theatre and workshops*, Carlisle: Cumbria County Council

Dadzie, Stella (2000) *Toolkit for Tackling Racism in Schools*, Stoke on Trent: Trentham Books

Daffé, Jane and Yvonne Kay, Judith Moore and Stella Nickolay (2005) *Integrating Global and Antiracist Perspectives within the Primary Curriculum*, City of Nottingham Education Department

Daily Telegraph (2006) 'Ruled by the politics of the playground', 8 April

Department for Education and Skills (2006a) *Bullying around Racism, Religion and Culture*, London: Department for Education and Skills, web-published at http://www.teachernet.gov.uk/_doc/10444/6562-DfES-Bullying.pdf (last accessed August 2008)

Department for Education and Skills (2006b) *Recording and Reporting Racist Incidents*, London: Department for Education and Skills

Department for Education and Skills (2004a) *Schools' Race Equality Policies: from issues to outcomes*, London: Department for Education and Skills

Department for Education and Skills (2004b) *Aiming High: understanding the needs of minority ethnic pupils in mainly white schools*, London: Department for Education and Skills

Doughty, Steve (2008) 'Children as young as three should be reported for 'racism', Government-funded group claims', *Daily Mail*, 7 July

Ealing Education Department (2003) *Preventing and Addressing Racism in Schools*, London Borough of Ealing

Edmiston, Brian (2008) *Mountains, Ships and Time-machines: making space for creativity and learning with dramatic inquiry in a primary school*, Durham: Creative Partnerships

European Commission on Racism and Intolerance (2002) *National Legislation to Combat Racism and Racial Discrimination*, Strasbourg: Council of Europe, 13 December

Evans, Oliver (2008) 'Racist incidents rise in south Bucks schools', *Free Bucks Press*, 11 June

Gaine, Chris (2005) *We're All White, Thanks: the persisting myth about 'white' schools*, Stoke on Trent: Trentham Books

Galtung, Johan (2004) *Transcend and Transform: an introduction to conflict work (peace by peaceful means)*, London: Pluto Press

Gluck Wood, Angela (2007) *What Do We Tell the Children? – confusion, conflict and complexity*, Stoke on Trent: Trentham Books

Hannam, Lewis (2007) 'Revealed: racism in schools', Channel Four News, 24 May, http://www.channel4.com/news/articles/society/education/revealed+racism+in+schools/529297 (last accessed July 2008)

Heffer, Simon (2006) 'Racists: we've got to catch them young', *Daily Telegraph*, 8 April

Hennessy, James (2007) Resources for hope: engaging with controversial issues through drama, in Claire and Holden eds (2007) *The Challenge of Teaching Controversial Issues*, Stoke on Trent: Trentham Books

Historical Association (2007) *Teaching Emotional and Controversial Issues 3-19*, London: The Historical Association

Hopkins, Belinda (2003) *Just Schools: a whole school approach to restorative justice*, London: Jessica Kingsley Publishing

Howe, Brian, and Katherine Covell eds (2007) *A Question of Commitment: children's rights in Canada*, Waterloo: Wilfrid Laurier University Press

Imran, Muhammad and Elaine Miskell (2003) *Citizenship and Muslim Perspectives: teachers sharing ideas,* London: Islamic Relief and Birmingham: Teachers in Development Education

Insted Consultancy (2007) *The Search for Common Ground: Muslims, non-Muslims and the UK media.* London: Greater London Authority, web-published at http://www.london.gov.uk/mayor/equalities/docs/commonground_report.pdf (last accessed August 2008)

Isal, Sarah (2005) *Preventing Racist Violence: work with actual and potential perpetrators*, London: Runnymede Trust

Johnson, Nick and Phil McCarvill (2007) *CRE Monitoring and Enforcement Plan: final report*, London: Commission for Racial Equality, archived at http://www.equalityhumanrights.com/Documents/Race/General%20advice%20and%20information/monitoring_and_enforcement_report_2005-7.pdf (last accessed August 2008)

Kaufman, Gershen and Lev Raphael, Pamela Espeland (1999) *Stick Up for Yourself: every kid's guide to personal power and positive self-esteem,* Minneapolis: Free Spirit Publishing

Keegan, John (2001) In this war of civilisations, the West will prevail, *Daily Telegraph*, 8 October

Khan, Omar (2002) *Perpetrators of Racist Violence and Harassment*, London: Runnymede Trust

Kick It Out (2007) *Schools' Resource Pack 2007-08*, London: Kick It Out

Kick It Out (2006) *Schools' Resource Pack*, London: Kick It Out

Knowles, Eleanor and Wendy Ridley (2006) *Another Spanner in the Works: challenging prejudice and racism in mainly white schools*, Stoke on Trent: Trentham Books

Kundnani, Arun (2004) In Memory of Blair Peach: an analysis of the changing face of racism, *Race Equality Teaching*, vol 22 no 3

Lane, Jane (2008) *Young Children and Racial Justice: taking action for racial equality in the early years*, London: National Children's Bureau

Leach, Fiona and Claudia Mitchell eds (2006) *Combating Gender Violence in and around Schools*, Stoke on Trent: Trentham Books

Lederach, John Paul (2003) *The Little Book of Conflict Transformation*, Intercourse PA: Good Books

Lemos, Gerard (2005) *The Search for Tolerance: challenging and changing racist attitudes and behaviour among young people*, York: Joseph Rowntree Foundation

Lewis, Miranda and Naomi Newman (2007) *Challenging attitudes, perceptions and myths, London: Commission on Integration and Cohesion*, Her Majesty's Stationery Office

Lovegrove, Emily (2006) *Help! I'm Being Bullied: ten practical strategies to stop bullying*, Pembrokeshire: Accent Press

Lynch, Lucy (2008) 'Warwickshire schools see drop in racist incidents', *Coventry Telegraph*, 29 April

MacLean, David (2008) 'Racist incidents in schools are falling', *Shields Gazette*, 4 June

Macpherson, William (1999) *The Stephen Lawrence Inquiry*, London: The Stationery Office

Malone, Carole (2006) 'Shame on the Playtime Police', *Sunday Mirror*, 9 April

Marshall, Tony (1999) *Restorative Justice: an overview*, London: Research Development and Statistics Directorate, Home Office

Maylor, Uvanney and Barbara Read, with Heather Mendick, Alistair Ross and Nicola Rollock (2007) *Diversity and Citizenship in the Curriculum: research review*, London: Department for Education and Skills, research brief RB819

Mirza, Heidi (2007) quoted in Hannam (2007), see above

Narain, Jaya (2006) 'A 'victory for common sense' as race charge is dropped against boy, 10', *Daily Mail*, 27 April

National Association of Schoolmasters and Union of Women Teachers (2006) *Tackling Prejudice-related Bullying*, London: NASUWT

Nesbitt, William (1971) *Interpreting the Newspaper in the Classroom: foreign news and world news*, New York: Foreign Policy Association

Office for Democratic Institutions and Human Rights with Yad Vashem (2007) *Addressing Antisemitism: why and how? A guide for educators*, Warsaw: ODIHR and Jerusalem: Yad Vashem

Ofsted (2008) *Children and Bullying: a report by the Children's Rights Director for England*, London: Office for Standards in Education

Ofsted (2005) *Race Equality in Education: good practice in schools and local education authorities*, London: Office for Standards in Education

Ofsted (2003) *Bullying: effective action in secondary schools*, London: Office for Standards in Education

Oliver, Christine and Mano Candappa (2003) *Tackling Bullying: listening to the views of children and young people*, London: Thomas Coram Research Unit

Olweus, Dan (1993) *Bullying at School: what we know and what we can do*, Oxford: Blackwell

Osler, Audrey (2008) Citizenship education and the Ajegbo report: re-imagining a cosmopolitan nation, *London Review of Education*, vol 6 no 1, March

Osler, Audrey and Hugh Starkey (2005) *Changing Citizenship: democracy and inclusion in education*, Maidenhead: Open University Press

Osler, Audrey and Marlene Morrison (2000) *Inspecting Schools for Race Equality: Ofsted's strengths and weaknesses*, London: Commission for Racial Equality and Stoke on Trent: Trentham Books

Parekh, Bhikhu (2008) *A New Politics of Identity: political principles for an interdependent world*, Basingstoke: Palgrave Macmillan

Philo, Greg and Mike Berry (2004) *Bad News from Israel*, London: Pluto Press

Pearce, Sarah (2005) *You Wouldn't Understand: white teachers in multiethnic classrooms*, Stoke on Trent: Trentham Books

Peters, Andrew Fusek (2005) Foreword to *National Anti-Bullying Poetry Competition: winners anthology,* London: Department for Education and Skills

Qualifications and Curriculum Authority (2007) *Meeting the Challenge: achieving equality for all*, London: Qualifications and Curriculum Authority

Pollard, Charles and Kenny Frederick, Graham Robb, Mel Stanley (2008) *Restorative Justice in Schools, Teachers* TV RSA Lectures, http://www.teachers.tv/video/27544 (last accessed June 2008)

Rees, Bethan (2003) *Promoting Racial Equality and Cultural Diversity*, Cambridge: Pearson Publishing

Richardson, Robin (2006) Classrooms and corridors: DfES advice on racist bullying in schools, *Race Equality Teaching*, vol 26 no 3, summer

Richardson, Robin (2004) *Here, There and Everywhere: belonging, identity and equality in schools*, Stoke on Trent: Trentham Books

Runnymede Trust (2003) *Complementing Teachers: a practical guide to promoting race equality in schools*, London: Granada Learning

Sardar, Ziauddin (2008) *The Language of Equality: a discussion paper*, Manchester: Equality and Human Rights Commission

Sawhney, Nitin (2004) Trust and betrayal, in *Cultural Breakthrough: the essays*, London: Voluntary Service Overseas

Sibbitt, Rae (1997) T*he Perpetrators of Racist Harassment and Racial Violence*, Research Study 176, London: Home Office

Sivanandan, A. (2001) *Poverty is the New Black, Race and Class* vol 43 no 6

Sivanandan, A (1980) Antiracist not multicultural education, *Race and Class* vol 22 no 1

Slack, James and Jaya Narain (2006) 'Slur on judge in schoolboy race case', *Daily Mail*, 8 April

Taylor, Philip and Christine Warner eds (2006) *Structure and Spontaneity: the process drama of Cecily O'Neill*, Stoke on Trent: Trentham Books

Theodore, Dylan (2004) *Coming Unstuck: guidance and activities for teaching about racism with 10 to 11-year-olds*, Winchester: Hampshire County Council

Thomas, Ronald Stuart (1973) *Laboratories of the Spirit*, London: Faber 1973

Troyna, Barry and Richard Hatcher (1992) *Racism in Children's Lives: a study of mainly white schools*, London: Routledge

Tynan, Kenneth (1957) in Tom Maschler ed (1957) *Declaration*, London: MacGibbon and Kee

van Dijk, Lutz and Barry Van Driel eds (2007) *Challenging Homophobia: teaching about sexual diversity,* Stoke on Trent: Trentham Books

van Driel, Barry ed (2004) *Confronting Islamophobia in Educational Practice*, Stoke on Trent: Trentham Books

Wanless, Peter (2006) *Getting It, Getting It Right: priority review of exclusion of black pupils*, London: Department for Education and Skills

Widdecombe, Anne (2006) 'Don't take playground tiffs into the courtroom', *Daily Express*, 12 April

Winston, Joe (1998) *Drama, Narrative and Moral Education: exploring traditional tales in the primary years*, London: Falmer Press

Womankind Worldwide (2007) *Challenging Violence, Changing Lives: gender on the UK education agenda, findings and recommendations*, London: Womankind Worldwide

York Consulting (2006) *Review of Guidance on Dealing with Racist Incidents: final report*, Edinburgh: Scottish Executive Education Department, http://www.scotland.gov.uk/Publications/ 2006/05/23155332/0 (last accessed July 2008)

Zehr, Howard (2002) *The Little Book of Restorative Justice*, Intercourse, PA: Good Books

Subject Index

Index of names